Richard Chamberlain

Richard Chamberlain

An Actor's Life

BARBARA SIEGEL & SCOTT SIEGEL

NEW ENGLISH LIBRARY

British Library Cataloguing in Publication Data

Siegel, Barbara
   Richard Chamberlain: an actor's life
   1. United States. Acting. Chamberlain, Richard, 1935–
   I. Title   II. Siegel, Scott
   792'.028'0924

   ISBN 0 450 50895 1

First published in Great Britain 1989

Reproduced by arrangement with
St. Martin's Press Inc., New York, USA.

Published by New English Library,
a hardcover imprint of Hodder and Stoughton,
a division of Hodder and Stoughton Ltd,
Mill Road, Dunton Green, Sevenoaks, Kent TN13 2YA
Editorial Office: 47 Bedford Square, London WC1B 3DP

Printed in Great Britain by St Edmundsbury Press Ltd,
Bury St Edmunds, Suffolk.

GLUCK RECEIVES DEDICATION!
Newsman Is Honored For Loyal Friendship
by Barbara Siegel & Scott Siegel

Future Pulitzer Prize winner and hard-driving
reporter Andrew ("Andy") M. Gluck received a
book dedication today for his brash charm, insight, and humor. Gluck known as a *continued
on page 886, column 1 . . .*

CONTENTS

ACKNOWLEDGMENTS

*W*e are indebted to the many actors, directors, and producers who worked with Richard Chamberlain and who were generous enough to share their thoughts, memories, and anecdotes about him. Among the actors, we'd like to offer special thanks for their invaluable contributions to Dina Merrill, Richard Kiley, Sylvia Miles, Fritz Weaver, Dorothy McGuire, and Pat Buttram.

We received particular insights from directors Richard Lester and Joseph Hardy, and to them we offer our heartfelt appreciation.

To producers Norman Felton and Douglas Benton, who were so instrumental in bringing *Dr. Kildare* to television, thank you so much for your fascinating personal recollections.

Of course, Richard Chamberlain's life hasn't been spent entirely in show business. We'd like to thank those people "who knew him when," such as Shelton L. Beatty and James Grant, for their rich recollections.

In addition to the many interviews that were conducted for the purpose of writing this book, we also relied upon the work of a great many journalists who have followed Richard Chamberlain's career throughout the years. There are far too many names to list, but we are grateful to them all for their helpful articles, interviews, and reviews.

And, finally, our warmest thanks and appreciation must go to Darcel Dillard for her splendid research. Her thorough, painstaking work was an enormous help to us, and she has our sincere gratitude.

INTRODUCTION

*F*or nearly thirty years, audiences all around the world have been calling Richard Chamberlain by his middle name. His first name is George, but neither he nor his family and friends have ever used it. There is something fitting about his hidden, forgotten first name, because Chamberlain has always been something of a mystery. The facts about him have been shrouded in a long career that has had three major phases, each one partially obliterating the life that existed beforehand. First there was the instant stardom of *Dr. Kildare*. Next came his unexpected triumph in *Hamlet* and his highly respected theater career in the classics. And then, finally, his reemergence on the tube as "King of the Miniseries."

Chamberlain has been constantly re-creating himself, growing, changing, evolving. It's an actor's job to shed his own identity and plunge into the soul of another character, and that job has suited Chamberlain very well. But for those millions of people who loved him as Kildare, respected him as Hamlet, and who now admire him as TV's preeminent actor, there is a desire to know more about this man, this image, known as Richard Chamberlain. It is our hope that this book will shed some light on that elusive subject.

1

CHILDHOOD TRAUMA

George Richard Chamberlain was born at Angelus Hospital in Beverly Hills, California, on March 31, 1935. He was the second son of Charles and Elsa Chamberlain. His father was a successful businessman who manufactured supermarket fixtures which he sold to food-store chains. His mother, however, was the power in the family. Both of his parents were of English ancestry but there was a strain of Cherokee Indian blood on his father's side, which explains Chamberlain's high cheekbones.

Richard grew up in one of America's wealthiest and most famous communities. His family was well to do, but that didn't mean that life for the young boy was easy and simple.

He had a horrible time in school as a child and it had a tremendous effect on his personality. He was far along in the Beverly Vista Grammar School before it was discovered that he was dyslexic. "The teacher would be holding up flash cards," Chamberlain painfully recalled, "and all the kids in the class would be shouting, 'Horse,' 'Cat,' 'Dog.' And all I saw were black smudges on a white background. I hated it." It wasn't until the fourth grade that he finally learned to read "when I found a teacher I liked."

Dyslexia is a condition that doesn't simply go away. "I still read very slowly," Chamberlain recently admitted. "I have a little voice inside my head that reads every word." The pain of being thought of as stupid throughout much of his early childhood still haunts him. "It's deeper than having freckles and getting kidded about it," he understated.

"I learned not to like myself somehow," he said. "So I grew up pretending to be somebody else. When you do that, your real self gets unhappy because it doesn't have any expression. In the beginning, I hardly ever knew when I was angry. I just didn't know because my object in life was to please people."

Children always seek approval, but Chamberlain needed it more than most kids. "I always feared rejection," he said. "I was afraid of not being liked. I did whatever I thought people expected of me . . .

"I found the pretense deadening," he continued. "The underlying assumption is that what you really are is not acceptable . . . it's taken me most of my life to untie that knot. It's not that I don't want to please now. I don't think actors ever get away from that. But the mania for pretending to be something I'm not has changed."

There were other problems besides the dyslexia. Chamberlain's father was a distant, aloof man who had a reputation as a perfectionist. Ironically, Chamberlain has been accused of these very same personality traits—but their ultimate similarities didn't draw them any closer together.

Richard might not have had a warm relationship with his father, but he respected him. "He never had a signed contract," the actor recalled. "Everyone trusted him. I picked up from him a sense of integrity." He also picked up the sure knowledge that he didn't want to work for his father. Before he became an actor, the elder Mr. Chamberlain offered him a job in the family business. Richard turned him down.

Many years later, before his dad passed away, Chamberlain played Wild Bill Hickok in Thomas Babe's play, *Fathers and Sons*. Chamberlain drew his inspiration for the role from his own father and invited him to see the show. The elder Mr. Chamberlain had little to say after the curtain came down. Nonetheless, Richard said, "He mellowed a lot in his last years. We got closer but never had the intimacy that I imagine would have been a real kind of resolution. In a way, that's too bad. In another way, well, okay, that's the way it was."

Then, of course, there were the normal problems of growing up. For instance, Chamberlain wore steel braces for several years to correct buck teeth. "Believe me," he said, flashing his now perfect smile, "every lunch was an adventure."

Richard wasn't the only handsome kid in the family. Douglas Benton, who was a story editor and later a producer of the *Dr. Kildare* series, met Bill Chamberlain, Richard's older brother, and said that he "was also a golden boy, and was just as good-looking as Dick and could have been an actor, too, I'm sure."

But there was only one actor in this family. And there was only one powerhouse: Elsa Chamberlain. "His mother was extremely strong and quite, quite bright," recalled Douglas Benton. She was used to having her way and didn't brook any interference. Yet Richard was clearly closer to her than he was to his father.

In the midst of his unhappy childhood, Chamberlain had his first taste of acting when he was eight years old. He played the title role in *The Pied Piper* in the third grade and fell in love with the stage. He never took it seriously, though, until his senior year of college. In between, he simply suffered . . .

"I hated school," he proclaimed. "I hated sports. I hated anything anyone told me to do. I hated to be told I'm not a man if I don't do them." This was hardly the image of the future Mr. Perfect, Dr. James Kildare.

Happily, Pomona College offered Chamberlain a new beginning.

2

TO PAINT OR
NOT TO PAINT

*P*omona College in Claremont, California, was known as "the Oxford of the Orange Belt." It was a small, private school with a strong tradition of upper-class education. Ostensibly, Chamberlain went there to study painting. He had shown some talent in that area and hoped to have a career as a commercial artist.

In a recent interview, his painting teacher at Pomona, James Grant, said, "He was quite talented as a painter. . . . He was one of half a dozen who stood out." When asked if he might have made it as a fine artist, Grant demurred, saying, "It's hard to say what would have happened to him." He insisted, nevertheless, that Chamberlain "had a good deal of talent and worked hard at it."

For his own part, Chamberlain didn't think he had a great future with a paintbrush and an easel. "I enjoyed it [painting], but I never was able to give myself completely to it," he recalled. "I had a good sense of design. Nothing inspired."

The inspiration that he was looking for didn't come from his painting, it came from the theater. Despite its small size, Pomona had already graduated two major Hollywood stars, Robert Taylor and Joel McCrea. It soon graduated three more talented men into show business: Will Hutchins (who starred in the TV series *Sugarfoot* and *Hey, Landlord!*), Kris Kristofferson, and Richard Chamberlain. Hutchins was in Chamberlain's class, and Kristofferson was just one year behind them. It was due, in fact, to Will Hutchins's urging that Chamberlain took a more active role in the school's theatrical life.

The drama teacher at Pomona was, in Chamberlain's own words, "A wonderful, frail old woman" who galvanized his interest in the classics. He thought the world of her. Many years later, when Chamberlain was starring in *Richard II* in Los Angeles, Shelton L. Beatty, the former dean of studies at Pomona, went backstage after the performance. "His [Chamberlain's] first question to me after we finished a very few pleasant remarks, was to ask how his drama teacher at Pomona was. And I said, 'Oh, Richard, she's in a nursing home over in Laverne. And there is nothing that could bring as much good health to her as a visit from you.' And he said, 'Give me the address. I'll go see her.' Well, about two weeks later a rich voice—the voice of his drama teacher—came over the line. 'Guess who came to see me yesterday and stayed two hours even though he was told he should leave after thirty minutes?'" Mr. Beatty proudly concluded, "It was Richard Chamberlain, of course."

Mr. Beatty remembered Chamberlain from his Pomona days and said that no one at the time would have guessed that he'd become a star. "They did not think of him as having great fire," he recalled. The folks at Pomona are not to be blamed for a lack of insight or perception. Chamberlain did relatively little acting at school until his senior year.

His first role in a college play was in *George Washington Slept Here*. Later, he appeared in school productions of *King Lear* (he had five lines of dialogue), *The Lady's Not for Burning* (a modest role), and George Bernard Shaw's *Arms and the Man*. It was in the last of these that he thought for the very first time, "Ah, I can act!"

Just because he could bring a character to life, however, didn't mean he was going to become an actor. That decision happened in a more private moment. "I moonlighted in the drama department," he explained. "I used to stay up [at school] on holidays and I would paint my ass off just to keep up . . . And I was up in this room in my senior year. I had a little room to myself—seniors had some privileges—and I could see Holmes Hall [home of the drama department] in the distance through this little window, and I thought, 'I don't want to be up here alone with this stupid white canvas driving me crazy. It's like sitting in front of a typewriter with a blank page—it's just too terrifying . . . I want to be down there with them. I want to be with people.' So. That's when I made the decision."

There was also a dark underpinning to his desire to act. It had nothing to do with entertaining people or bringing great works alive on stage. It was a deeply personal reason. "Some people grow up fast," he explained. "I didn't. I was quite late in growing up. Why, I don't know. I just stayed in semi-hibernation for a long, long time. I was extremely shy. In college I was a hermit. I sat in my little room and I painted pictures. I was in some sort of cocoon . . .

"Then I discovered acting. The stage seemed like a place where you could escape from the cocoon. It seemed like a place where you could be free. Free to express your emotions . . . free to move . . . free to shout. It seemed like a way to have fun without getting involved in real life."

He paused.

"But you can't really avoid life by moving into a larger cocoon, can you?" he said. "Sooner or later you're forced to try to discover reality—to discover what's real and what's phony."

Chamberlain has been on that quest for a very long time now.

3

THE SHORT STRUGGLE

*C*hamberlain graduated from Pomona College in 1956. He had already chosen acting as a career, but Uncle Sam had other plans for him, at least for the next two years. He was drafted and sent to Korea.

The war had been over for several years and his sixteen-month tour of duty overseas was not fraught with danger. He worked as an infantry company clerk, and the closest he came to dying, he said, was when "I nearly died of boredom." The time he spent in the army was "totally opposed to my nature." Yet his stint in the army had a certain perverse positive effect on him. "I think what I got out of it," he said, "was a feeling that I could survive anything."

Chamberlain was honorably discharged from the service with the rank of sergeant in 1958. He might have looked terribly young and innocent when he first appeared on TV, but he was a veteran who had earned his stripes.

The idea of becoming an actor hadn't paled while he was in the service. He plunged into acting classes, but with very little success. After just one session at Lee Strasberg's Actors Studio in New York, Chamberlain quit. "They all took themselves too seriously," he recalled. "I would laugh at myself before I went that far." Back in California, he studied with Jeff Corey, a highly respected acting teacher. Chamberlain learned a great deal, but he didn't make the kind of strides he had hoped for. He later conceded that he was "too frightened to do the kind of personal investigation he [Corey] encouraged."

All of this happened over a relatively short period of time. It was, nonetheless, a very discouraging stretch for the aspiring actor. Having grown up in Beverly Hills, he knew more about the business than most other young actors who arrived in Los Angeles by the busload every day. "I've always known the odds, known the amount of luck, the chance of being in the right place at the right time," he said. "I've seen too many beach boys in Santa Monica not to realize that there are many more beach boys than there are movie stars."

He was committed to the profession and he did the kinds of things other struggling actors had to do to survive. "I worked as a box boy at Ralph's Market on Wilshire Boulevard, waited on tables, worked as a chauffeur, collected unemployment checks. I didn't have much money. My mother owned a small percentage in an oil well that only produced enough oil to send me through college before it ran dry." More to the point, in late 1958 he was twenty-four years old, an army veteran, and no longer his parents' responsibility.

He was going to have to make it on his own.

"It's such an elusive profession—before you've ever had a job it's just a dream, nobody around you believes it's really possible," Chamberlain lamented. "Unless you've got something like a mania inside, most people give it up, or get into that very bad position of taking any little jobs they can find, hoping against hope."

Chamberlain had the mania inside. It was early 1959 and

his career was worse than stalled; he hadn't even gotten the motor started.

"Millions of people auditioned me, nobody hired me," he remembered. He felt he knew what his problem was: "I didn't read [audition] well." That may have been part of it, but what he really lacked was a strong advocate in the business. He needed an agent, and he ultimately found just the right person to handle him. Her name was Monique James. She was a very bright, energetic agent who worked for MCA. Monique had a reputation for finding and developing new talent, but she outdid herself when she discovered Richard Chamberlain.

Once she took over his career, things began to happen very quickly. In the second half of 1959 he had his first job, a small part in a *Gunsmoke* episode. It was half of a day's work, but it was a credit. A handful of other parts soon followed on shows such as *The Deputy* and *Mr. Lucky*.

A couple of small movie roles came his way, too. His feature film debut was in the programmer, *The Secret of the Purple Reef* (1960), starring Jeff Richards. This was not what you would call an all-star cast. Along with Richards, the players were Peter Falk (long before anyone knew who he was), Margia Dean, and several other unknowns. Chamberlain had a fairly substantial role in the film, which he later referred to as "Easily the worst movie ever made, or at least the most boring."

Not long after his experience with *Secret of the Purple Reef*, he landed a role in the MGM Western, *A Thunder of Drums* (1961). It was a decent cavalry movie that starred Richard Boone and George Hamilton, with Charles Bronson and Arthur O'Connell in major supporting roles along with Chamberlain. If nothing else, Chamberlain looked good in uniform. He knew how to ride horses and that knowledge served him well in a good many films, beginning with this one.

If no one else was impressed, at least MGM was. Later that year they signed him up to a long-term contract.

In the meantime, though, producer Douglas Benton had a memorable look at Chamberlain's growth as an actor before the rest of America took notice of him. "The first time I ever met him, really, was when he did a small part for me in an episode of the old *Thriller* TV show that we made with Boris Karloff," he said. "He was very green. Raw. He had only been acting for six or seven months. We had him in this little part mainly because of Monique's insistence. And I thought to myself, another pretty boy. He doesn't seem strong enough to be a leading man . . . A couple of years later, when I went over to work on *Dr. Kildare,* I was dumbfounded at how much he had learned."

The highly respected actor Raymond Massey, who had starred for decades on stage and screen, and who would later play Dr. Gillespie on *Kildare,* also had an early look at Chamberlain's acting skills. Just by chance, they worked together in an episode of *Alfred Hitchcock Presents* entitled "Road Hog." Chamberlain played Raymond Massey's son. It was a meeting which would later prove crucial in the young actor's career.

4

IS THERE A DOCTOR IN THE HOUSE?

*G*ood looks can take an actor only so far. Talent certainly helps if he wants any sort of long-term success. But the one thing every actor craves is luck. And Richard Chamberlain's incredible lucky streak was about to begin. At the start, however, his luck seemed anything but good.

It appeared as is he was on the verge of a big success when he was signed to play the lead role in a TV pilot for Metro-Goldwyn-Mayer. That project, however, wasn't *Dr. Kildare,* it was a comic Western series called *The Paradise Kid* in which Chamberlain played a Yale graduate who ends up out on the frontier. The pilot was never aired. Chamberlain's big chance had apparently come to nothing. He did, however, get a shot at the role of the bridegroom in the TV series *Father of the Bride,* but "they didn't like me for the role," admitted Chamberlain. MGM had him under contract, but they didn't know what to do with him.

Enter Mr. Norman Felton. He had been hired in 1960

by MGM to become their Director of TV. "I also had a contract with them to do a pilot film, hopefully leading to a series for Arena Productions, my own company." Felton had considerable experience in radio as both a producer and director of dramatic medical series. For several years he had been trying to do the same kind of show on TV. "At that time," Felton recalled, "the networks felt that it wasn't a favorable thing to do a medical series where the audience would have to see people who were ill all the time. So it was difficult. When I went to MGM, however, on my first project for my own company, I decided to develop a medical series, and MGM said that if I did, would I use the title of *Dr. Kildare*? I agreed."

MGM, of course, owned the rights to *Dr. Kildare*, having made an enormously successful series of motion pictures about the young physician from 1938 through 1947. Lew Ayres and later Van Johnson played Kildare in that series. Lionel Barrymore had the role of the crusty old Dr. Leonard Gillespie, the intern's mentor, in all of the MGM vehicles. It was not an unreasonable hope on MGM's part to duplicate the success of *Dr. Kildare* on TV. After all, if it worked once, it might certainly work again. And, besides, the new TV series would have the advantage of instant name recognition among older viewers.

After Felton made a development deal with NBC to develop a half-hour pilot film ("NBC didn't want to put more money into it than a half-hour pilot at that time," said Felton), he set about to cast the project. "I had already talked to Raymond Massey, who was a good friend whom I had directed many times, about playing the role of the older doctor. And he agreed to do that. But after interviewing many people for the principal role, someone at MGM said, 'You might consider a young man that we have under contract, Richard Chamberlain.' I said, 'Well, I don't know him, but I'd like to see some film.'"

Chamberlain's bad luck in *The Paradise Kid* was about to change. Felton saw both the failed pilot and the young actor's potential. "I must be honest," said Felton, "the work that I saw was not representative of his best work. Of course," he added, "I didn't know that at the time." In any event, Chamberlain was now in the running for the title role in *Dr. Kildare*.

According to Douglas Benton, a man with a wry sense of humor who worked as a story editor on the show for three years and later produced the last sixty *Dr. Kildare* episodes, there was very stiff competition for the role of Kildare. At the end, said Benton, "There were three finalists: James Franciscus, Dick Chamberlain, and another actor who has subsequently disappeared, I think, into Utah; his name was Robert Redford. They all looked alike; Redford is blond and blue-eyed, Franciscus is blond and blue-eyed, and Dick Chamberlain is kind of a sandy blond. If you line them up, they all look alike except that Dick is half a head taller than the other two. As a matter of fact, we had Redford as a guest star one time, and Norman [Felton] was very upset about it. He said, 'Jesus Christ, I can't tell one from the other. You should have put them in white and black hats.'"

When asked why Chamberlain was chosen over the other two, Benton paused for a moment and said, "Raymond Massey was really the reason Dick got the job as Dr. Kildare. He had worked with Dick in an Alfred Hitchcock show, and he had been impressed with how hard Dick tried, and the fact that he was a gentleman. Raymond put great stock in good manners. And I think that's really why Dick got the job."

At this point, however, it was still another pilot project, just like *The Paradise Kid*. There was no commitment by NBC to air the show.

E. Jack Newman had written the original half-hour pilot,

and he was asked to expand it to a full one-hour show. Boris Sagal was hired to direct. The one-hour *Dr. Kildare* film was titled "Twenty-Four Hours." Norman Felton explained, "It was really twenty-four hours in the life of an intern. We started filming on a Thursday and on Friday morning I saw the dailies. As often happens in filmmaking, the scenes with the fewest actors in them are frequently filmed first in order to avoid carrying a lot of actors who are not yet in the story. So we were doing the first-day scenes between Raymond Massey and Richard Chamberlain. When I saw those dailies on the Friday morning, they were superb. They just were so exciting.

"I called the head of programming at the network who happened to be in Hollywood at the time, though he was based in New York. I said, 'You've got to see this film before you go back.' It's one thing of course to make a pilot film and another to have the network put on a series. . . . It was late in the season, and I knew they were already making up their plans for the following year. I wanted to get that [*Dr. Kildare*] on the air. He said, 'Here it is Friday afternoon and tomorrow at one o'clock I'm flying back to New York. I don't know how I can see it.' I said, 'Come out Saturday morning.'

"He came in the rain, I remember. His name was David Levy. He and I sat in this projection room by ourselves. I ran the dailies. And he was as excited as I was. He turned to me after the lights came up and he said, 'Norman, that's going to be on our schedule for next year. At least I'm going to do everything I can to see that it is.'"

True to his word, the NBC man built interest in the new *Dr. Kildare* series with his aggressive enthusiasm for the show. The network reserved a spot on the 1961 schedule for the medical program, pending their reaction to the pilot. When filming was finished and a rough cut of the show was edited together, Felton sent it to New York.

The NBC brass loved it. *Dr. Kildare* was about to become the new hit sensation of the 1961 TV season. And an unknown actor with precious little acting experience was about to become one of TV's biggest stars.

5

SHE KISSED
HIS LIPS OFF

*A*ccording to Richard Chamberlain, his image as TV's Dr. Kildare has long since faded into obscurity. "Nobody walks up to me on the street and asks about it," he said. "I think most people who watched it are dead."

Hardly. His biggest fans during the early 1960s were teenage girls and now, as women in their late thirties and early forties, they form the core of his vast miniseries audience.

The intensity of Chamberlain's celebrityhood during those heady years of *Dr. Kildare* cannot be overestimated. At the peak of his popularity, Chamberlain was receiving twelve thousand fan letters per month, surpassing the previous record set by Clark Gable's fans in 1940, the year after *Gone With the Wind*.

At first, Chamberlain was blissfully unaware of his burgeoning fame. "It was only when I went East on a promotion tour for the series, meeting the press and so on, that I became aware that I was mighty well known," he said. "And it went to my head a little. I got cocky and smart with that adulation, being treated as if I had dropped from on high and was different from other mortals.

"Luckily, I had some old and good friends in New York. . . . Those friends were great at pricking balloons. And boy, was I a balloon! They soon cut me down to size. And I haven't forgotten it. It was the most salutary thing that could have happened to me, because it made me realize that this sort of fame is so temporary, so unimportant. It wasn't me they [the fans] were interested in. It was me as Kildare."

The fans were more than "interested" in Chamberlain. They were wild about him. In 1962 he made the mistake of appearing at Baltimore's annual "I Am an American Day" parade, and half a million people turned out, a gathering far in excess of any other year in the parade's twenty-three-year history. The massive crowd soon broke through police barricades and Chamberlain had to be put on a boat in the harbor in order to be saved from a surging mob of adoring fans.

The most telling evidence of Chamberlain's appeal to prepubescent teenage girls during the height of *Dr. Kildare* is best illustrated by the memory of a prominent female psychologist who said, "I learned how to kiss by using a poster of Richard Chamberlain." Then she laughed and added, "I kissed his lips off."

Of course, young girls weren't his entire audience. Children wrote to him. ("I'm just learning to write. Please send me a picture. So there will be no slip-up, the address at the bottom is written by Mama.") And older girls wrote to him, too. ("I want to come out to California to visit you. Please send me money.")

The young, hard-core fans who approached Chamberlain as part of a crowd or through the mail were often rather bold. But if they were ever actually lucky enough to talk to him in person, they were remarkably respectful. "The teenagers tend to call me Mr. Chamberlain," said the actor in the early 1960s. "I think the character of Kildare keeps them sort of subdued. I mean, I'm not a rock 'n' roll singer or a private eye or anything like that."

As Chamberlain suggested, the character of Kildare had been put on a pedestal by the public. *Dr. Kildare*—and particularly Chamberlain—had made an enormous impact on a nation hungry for a new kind of hero.

Dr. Kildare premiered on September 28, 1961, and ran for five full seasons. There was no slow climb in the ratings. The show was a winner virtually from the very start. By the end of its first season, it was ranked as the ninth most popular series on TV. To be frank, however, the show's success wasn't due to Chamberlain's thespian skills. There were strong stories, top-notch direction, and excellent guest stars to help out the fledgling actor.

Because Chamberlain played an intern learning the medical ropes during the first two years of the show's run, a certain amount of insecurity and hesitancy by the actor came across as perfectly in character for Kildare. While professional actors weren't fooled, the general public found Chamberlain perfectly believable in the role. And most amusing of all, so did his mother. "Oddly enough," Elsa Chamberlain candidly admitted, "I do sometimes get the feeling Dick is a doctor. I think it's because this part suits him more than anything else he has ever played. He's more convincing than he's ever been before. For once, I can sit back and enjoy his shows. I'm relaxed. It's almost as though I were watching somebody else's son, not mine. A casual friend of mine, I've heard, turned to her husband right after watching the show last week and said flatly, 'He's not an actor, he's a doctor.'"

Chamberlain was no doubt flattered by that kind of sentiment; it meant he was doing his job well. Yet he was troubled because "People in America hold doctors in a special kind of reverence. It's a reverence not generally extended to actors. Sometimes," he ruefully conceded, "I feel like an imposter."

Ah, but what a handsome imposter. There was no question that the six-foot-one, 175-pound actor's looks added immeasurably to the show's popularity. There was something else, however, behind the show's enormous success. Chamberlain was playing a new kind of character on TV. After a decade of Westerns on the tube, the emergence of a young, clean-cut, handsome young doctor was a breath of fresh air. Chamberlain's Kildare mirrored the changing times. John Kennedy had just been elected president, and the youth culture was coming into its own. Kennedy had brought idealism back into vogue and the image of the selfless, dedicated doctor was a perfect match for the age of the Peace Corps. In other words, the time was ripe for James Kildare.

The only problem was that Chamberlain, himself, wasn't ripe as an actor.

Accomplished performers who guest-starred on the series saw for themselves that TV's hottest male star was no Marlon Brando. The highly acclaimed Broadway and TV actor Richard Kiley was among them. Kiley, who later starred in Broadway shows such as *Man of La Mancha* and on TV in productions such as the critically praised series *A Year in the Life,* appeared on *Dr. Kildare.* He also costarred with Chamberlain in *The Thorn Birds* (for which he won an Emmy). He has seen Chamberlain's growth and change. Back during the *Kildare* days, Kiley reports, "He was a very tentative young guy who really wasn't terribly good . . . he was a little bit wooden . . . very green."

If Chamberlain has a reputation among his peers for anything, it's for his hard work. He might have been green, but he was dedicated to improving. Douglas Benton tells a story that illustrates the point. "We booked James Mason to play a guest role in a multipart *Dr. Kildare*," he explained. "The first day on the set, Mr. Mason . . . was so overwhelming, so powerful, that when Dick started to respond, his mouth just opened and nothing came out. The director said, 'Would you like to try it again, Dick?' And he said, 'No, I'm just not up to this today. I have to go back and regroup. But tomorrow I'll have it.' And sure enough, early the next morning Mr. Mason gave his powerful, stirring speech, and Dick came right back and gave him as good as he got."

Fritz Weaver, who later played Thomas Hart Benton, Richard Chamberlain's father-in-law in *Dream West,* also guest-starred on *Dr. Kildare* in the early 1960s. He recalled that Chamberlain "would disappear at lunch and have a singing lesson. I can remember being *terribly* impressed. There weren't many actors who did that out in cuckoo-land. I always believed in the importance of singing to actors, and I thought to myself, how does he know that at his age? It took me ten years to find out how important that is."

Chamberlain not only continued to take singing lessons, he also studied fencing, as well as dance, despite a killing schedule on *Kildare* that included shooting up to eighteen hours a day, six days a week. In that earlier era of TV programming, a one-year series commitment meant thirty-two shows per season, not the present twenty-six. But Chamberlain knew from the start that he didn't want to stand in place. *Kildare* was a great opportunity for him but he never saw it as the culmination of a life's dream. He wanted desperately to improve because he knew someday *Kildare* would end and he didn't want to end with it.

Douglas Benton said, "He's a workaholic. He may be gentle, pleasant, and easygoing, but he's a monomaniac. When he sets a goal, he doesn't let anything deter him. He goes right for it; it becomes *the* thing that he wants."

Chamberlain has made no pretense about it. What he wants—what he has always wanted—was to become an exceptional actor. During the *Kildare* years, however, he had to be content with merely being a star. The ironic twist was that both MGM and NBC thought that Raymond Massey was going to be the real star of the show. After all, he was a well-known, highly respected actor with a long and distinguished career. Chamberlain was an inexperienced unknown.

If Massey became jealous of the younger actor, he never showed it. And it wasn't because Massey was such a sweet old man. He wasn't. "He was full of himself," recalled Benton. "He knew who he was and he could be a little testy, and we all got the razor edge of his tongue from time to time. But no matter how difficult he got—and he was in his late sixties and early seventies—Dick always took it so beautifully. He'd just smile and defer to the old man. Obviously, Massey just loved him. They really got along. There was never one harsh word between the two of them."

"To me," said Chamberlain, "he was like a second father. I wasn't getting on with my own father too well at that time. . . . He seemed to step in and fill that gap. He was so kind to me and so supportive. . . . He never—even in the beginning—never once condescended to me."

Massey and Chamberlain had a combination teacher/ student and father/son relationship. But above all else, they were genuine friends. "He and Massey used to have a lot of private jokes," said Benton. "They'd get in the middle of a scene and then break up and nobody would know what they were amused at."

Not all of the jokes were private. One of the most memorable gags on the *Kildare* set occurred when Massey made his entrance into a scene made up as Abraham Lincoln (he had starred in the hit 1940 film, *Abe Lincoln in Illinois*).

Massey took a great deal of pride in his young protégé's early success. And the elder actor lived long enough (he died in 1983) to see that his belief in Chamberlain had been right on the mark.

6

ON-THE-JOB TRAINING

*R*ichard Chamberlain is not the type to throw his weight around, and that pattern was established from the very beginning of his *Dr. Kildare* stint. When shooting for the series began, the guard at the MGM gate reportedly wouldn't let Chamberlain in without calling the studio for clearance. The young actor was so unassuming that this continued for eight days with Chamberlain making no complaint.

This shy nature continued throughout the first year of the show, even though he had quickly become a bona fide media sensation. It was reliably reported that he criticized nary a script nor a scene during the first full year of shooting. It was all so new to him that he hardly felt he was in a position to know what was right or wrong even though he had the star clout to make plenty of changes. He even admitted that in his first year on the show he "did a lot of faking."

"When he began in *Kildare*," a friend recalled, "he was so darned polite that he'd take off his hat to the camera, and bow to the boom. He was nervous and uncertain, but he had the great gift of repose when he was working. That was the quality of keeping his face still when all around were moving theirs like mad, and that's what made him click."

When he began feeling more comfortable on the show, he graciously gave the credit to his producers, directors, writers, and fellow actors—particularly Raymond Massey. "I'm a group project," he would say. Later, however, with his confidence growing, Chamberlain became more assertive on the set. He even complained publicly about the way actors were treated, saying, "An actor, you know, is supposed to be the most stupid creature there is. They don't want you to think or say anything or change in any way. They don't even like to have you see the rushes—afraid you might get ideas."

Chamberlain *did* have ideas. And he wasn't shy about expressing them. But he never threw tantrums. "He was certainly no Sean Penn," said producer Douglas Benton with a laugh. Benton went on to say, "Shooting a weekly TV series is long and hard work. You can't help but be irritable. Believe me, I worked with Dick Boone and Peter Falk and I can tell you, there are times . . . but you never saw that side with Dick. If you talked to him then, he was very grateful for the opportunity. I mean it made him a celebrity; he was the favorite actor in Buckingham Palace at that time. The Royal Family would come sit down around the telly and watch *Dr. Kildare*."

The show's creator, Norman Felton, echoed his producer, saying, "He always came prepared. . . . He knew his character very well as time went on—probably better than anyone. He was usually right in his criticism. . . . Although there is a lot of truth to the fact the he was, in many ways, a gentle person and a caring person, when it came to the character and his place in the story, he did not back away if he felt that it had to be challenged. He wouldn't let go of it. He would talk to the director or the producer until a scene was reworked . . . he was very dogged and didn't let go. And he was respected and admired for that very reason. I had directors come to me and say, 'I wasn't sure that he was really right in that scene in the way that we redeveloped it, but he *was* right.' And he [the director] said, 'You know, you couldn't talk him out of what he believed.'"

Chamberlain not only impressed his bosses, he also impressed the show's guest stars, most of whom came to the series as seasoned professionals. They may not have been wowed by his acting at the time, but they often thought very highly of him. Fritz Weaver was no exception. "There was this squeaky-clean boy who had taken America by storm," he recently recalled. "Everybody was naturally very curious about him and I was astounded. I didn't know how old he was and all I could see was incredible composure. I've seen lots of young kids come up and go down very fast because they can't handle it. And here is this boy with a smile of inneffable patience on his face, handling everything as if he had been doing it for twenty-five years. . . . I could name some names of people who made enemies right and left because all the power went to their heads, but this boy never did that. He was just as sweet as he could be."

When asked about his seeming lack of a fiery temper, Chamberlain admitted that he rarely allowed anyone to see him get angry. Much later, during the filming of *The Thorn Birds,* he would break his hand on the set while in a rage, but during the *Kildare* series, he would find a quiet, secluded place and "just sort of turn purple and yell at the wall."

His emotional self-discipline and his desire to excel as an actor were palpable. "The boy has strength," Raymond Massey told a reporter. "He listens. He is stage-struck, not Chamberlain-struck. I took him to dinner once with Jack

Hawkins, that fine British actor, and Dick just sat there with his jaw hanging, drinking in everything Hawkins said."

Chamberlain not only listened to Hawkins's words of wisdom, he also learned how to listen as an actor. One mark of a good actor is whether or not he can hold audience attention in a scene even if he isn't speaking. The ability to be fully involved as a listener—to react without speaking—not only adds texture to a scene, it often improves everyone else's performance, as well. Suzanne Pleshette, who guest-starred on the award-winning *Kildare* episode, "A Shining Image," made a point of saying, "He listens instead of just worrying about which is his good side."

Douglas Benton concurred. He recalled a conversation he once had with Charles Laughton, who said that the best screen actor who ever lived was Gary Cooper because he had the ability to listen as well as possessing a glorious voice. In the course of watching Chamberlain work, Benton realized that "he has those two virtues; he's the best listener and he has a plummy, resonant, reassurring baritone voice that just reaches right out of the screen and grabs women by the throat."

If his voice grabbed women by the throat, then his face squeezed them by the throat till they were breathless. It was ironic, however, that Chamberlain wasn't as thrilled by his good looks as were his panting female fans. Looking at the lined and expressive visage of Raymond Massey on the *Kildare* set, he was once heard to mutter, "I wish I had a face like that."

There was nothing facetious in the remark. He knew he was handsome but he simply didn't trust the public reaction to his appearance. "It was just incredible to be suddenly so desirable," he said. "It certainly hadn't happened in high school—adulation from the girls on such a scale—and gradually it was a realization that the good looks were some kind of handicap, were limiting."

And he meant it, too. "Look at my face," he once demanded of a reporter. "It is a *nice* face. I'm not displeased with it, but it's the face of a male ingenue. You know, Raymond Massey and I were doing a gag on the set the other day. We made false noses for ourselves. Well, I looked in the mirror with my false nose on. It was so wonderful to have a strong, prominent, powerful feature. I do so hope that my face will acquire character as it grows older. I suppose it will if *I* do."

The character he hoped he might develop was already very much in evidence simply by virtue of his having made that statement. And another guest star on *Kildare,* Anne Francis, confirmed it when she said, "Dick is a very unusual young actor. He has dignity and a sense of integrity, both as an actor and as a person. So many of the others seem to be just prototypes of each other. It's refreshing to work with someone who doesn't feel it necessary to take on patterns that aren't his own."

The patterns Richard Chamberlain established in both his personal and professional lives during the early 1960s were definitely singular. It would have been very easy for him to do what so many other young stars have done and simply revel in his success. It wasn't his way. He went to a premiere and saw firsthand the nastier side of being a star. "They kept grabbing me for pictures with people like Tuesday Weld—I'd never met her—and I got the uncomfortable feeling I was being used as one of the members of the Hollywood 'younger set,' the party-goers," he said. "I'm not. I want no part of it."

Nor did he want to live and die with the role of Dr. Kildare. "Doing something like *Kildare* for two or three years, if we last that long, is both good and bad," he explained to an interviewer after the show's first full season. "You can get typed so fast. And they pick up a new face in this business, use it, wear it out in a hurry and discard it."

A studio executive said, "Kildare—he's every mother's

dreamboat. And no one wants a dreamboat with tar on its bottom. So you've got to keep the series clean." Keeping it "clean" also meant keeping the character of Kildare as pure as possible. And that rankled Chamberlain. He complained that Kildare was "a square. . . . He's noble, true, brave . . . a boy scout. He does things that I would never do. There's an episode . . . where Kildare gets angry—angry, mind you—at a nurse who won't attend her father's funeral. This is nonsense. I wouldn't get involved like that in people's lives. Kildare is always butting in!"

Nonetheless, he didn't opt to leave the confines of Blair General Hospital. And he had good reasons to stick with the series despite the fact that he did, indeed, become typed as a goody two-shoes. "The show served as a kind of basic training for me as an actor," he explained. He later added, "The series . . . gave me the experience to know how much I could draw out of myself, and to economize in expressing it. It was also very useful in making me adaptable. We had dozens of directors during the run, and some were pretty good, and there were also a lot of excellent guest stars in the later stages of the show. I'd have had to be very stupid not to learn from them all."

Beyond the valuable experience he gained during those five years on *Kildare,* he also appreciated the practical importance of his star status. "I'm an actor," he said simply and directly. "I want as much success as I can get, in much the same manner as a baseball player wants base hits. Stardom is infinitely more valuable than I'd ever hoped it would be simply because it has given me a chance to mature as an actor. And I'll tell you this. I certainly would miss the whole thing if it suddenly were to disappear."

He had his stardom and his actor's boot camp, but he didn't have the riches most people would have expected given his gargantuan popularity. True, MGM tore up his old contract when *Dr. Kildare* took off into the stratosphere, but they replaced it with a new seven-year escalating salary that was still peanuts compared to that of other popular stars. For instance, in 1965, his final year as Kildare, he made the relatively small sum of $60,000 for his work on the series. Other TV actors who had far less drawing power than Chamberlain were often making three or four times his salary. In addition, he never earned a penny in residuals when *Kildare* went into reruns. "Looking back," he says of MGM, "I see that I could have gotten a lot more money out of them. . . . I suppose I could have demanded a new contract, or started fainting on the set or run off to New York until they gave me a better deal. But I was so green I didn't do it. Certainly, I didn't come out of the series a millionaire."

Chamberlain, however, was never the kind of man to dwell on the past. Even while *Kildare* was in production, he was planning for his future. He lived very modestly, saving his money in order to bankroll his career after the inevitable day when *Kildare* was canceled. "I've always lived in an un-grandiose way," he said, "and I guess I'm used to it. For an actor, money is power. It lets him pick and choose."

Despite being a born and bred southern Californian—traditionally the most car-conscious humans on earth—Chamberlain's automobile was not a flashy, expensive car. Douglas Benton recalled seeing him at MGM shortly after joining the show. "He came off the sound stage and there was this Rolls Royce sitting there and I assumed it was his car because he was the star of the show. He went past it and got into this old beat-up gray Peugot that looked like the paint was peeling off of it. David Victor [the producer] was with me, and I said, 'Jesus, if that's his car, who owns the Rolls?' And he said, 'Oh, Raymond, of course.'"

Chamberlain eventually splurged and bought a Fiat 1200

sports car, but he saved money on rent by living in a studio apartment on the top floor of a small house in the Hollywood hills. It was his home before he became a star and he continued to live there for many years after becoming TV's most famous physician.

He was not, however, TV's only physician. . . .

7

JAMES KILDARE VERSUS BEN CASEY

*F*our days after *Dr. Kildare* was first broadcast, ABC countered with their own doctor show, *Ben Casey*, starring Vince Edwards. Both series proved to be major hits but their audiences didn't entirely overlap. *Kildare* was shown on Thursday nights between 8:30 and 9:30 P.M. (Eastern Daylight Time), and appealed to a much younger audience than *Ben Casey*, which aired Monday nights for one hour beginning at 10:00 P.M. (Eastern Daylight Time).

It's undoubtedly a gross overgeneralization, yet it seems somehow fair to say that there were three kinds of people in the United States during the early 1960s: *Dr. Kildare* fans, *Ben Casey* fans, and people who didn't own a TV. Edwards was the "sexy, dangerous man." Chamberlain was the "safe, nice boy." Older teenagers and women were aroused by Vince Edwards's hairy chest and angry, hot-tempered acting style. The younger set found Chamberlain's "prettiness" sexy in a non-threatening way and his sincerity only made him all the more perfect. To put it another way, Vince Edwards was someone older teens and women fantasized about having a torrid affair with, but Richard Chamberlain was someone girls (and plenty of women) wanted to marry. The raging debate among teen-age girls concerning which of the two was more desirable can still be resurrected today among women of the appropriate age at the mention of either actor's name.

The two shows had a remarkably similar run. They both lasted five years, with the ABC series being canceled a mere five months before *Kildare*. It's generally assumed that *Kildare* was always the front runner in popularity, but that wasn't so. In 1963, *Ben Casey* was the number seven show for the year, overtaking the eleventh-ranked *Dr. Kildare*. Most people believed that *Kildare* was always more popular because Chamberlain was, himself, a more popular actor than Vince Edwards—at least insofar as these things can be measured. For instance, according to John Javna in his book, *Cult TV*, the post office delivered roughly three times the fan mail to Richard Chamberlain than they dumped at the door of Vince Edwards. Perhaps more to the point, Chamberlain's core audience of two million teens was young, impressionable, and ever so youthfully enthusiastic.

The two actors were very much aware of each other. Sometimes, to a fault. For instance, a reporter witnessed a scene in one episode where Kildare was supposed to report to Dr. Gillespie about a patient named Ben Rainey. Chamberlain made his entrance and announced, "I came to see you about Ben Casey." The actors and crew burst into laughter. End of scene. Take two.

"We discuss that show a lot around here," Chamberlain admitted in an interview during his TV series heyday. "I imagine they discuss us, too. In fact I'd like to go over on their lot and meet them." Once, he even went so far as to playfully suggest that he'd "love to play Ben Casey. I'm dying to make the switch. It tickles my sense of humor. It would be great if I could do it for even one show. At the same time, maybe Vince Edwards could take a crack at portraying Dr. Kildare." Of course, he was only joking, but it clearly indicated how closely associated the two shows really were.

Many years later, Chamberlain conceded, "Actually, I rather liked *Ben Casey;* it had a toughness about it. We may not want to admit it, but hospitals are more like the one on *Ben Casey* than the one on *Dr. Kildare.*"

Nonetheless, while the two rivals knew one another intimately by reputation, they made no special effort to become friends. "Vince is a fine actor," said Chamberlain with his customary graciousness. But in an example of his studied aloofness, he also admitted, "I don't know him very well. We've met briefly at several public functions."

Chamberlain once made a point of saying that he didn't think that the two parts were at all similar. "Casey is older, more experienced," he explained. "Kildare is still young and green."

And that wasn't the only difference. "There were certain advantages, perhaps, that we had over the *Ben Casey* series, Norman Felton explained. "As an intern and later a resident, he [Kildare] would serve on all services. . . . He would have to serve for a year on surgical, obstetrics, all phases of being trained as a general physician. So the scope of our stories could be as wide as the various services in a hospital." In other words, there was a greater variety of plots available to *Kildare* than to *Ben Casey,* whose medical stories were generally limited to his neurosurgery specialty.

Because Kildare could go almost anywhere for a good story, a few truly splendid episodes were produced, the most memorable of which was a multipart show about epilepsy titled "Tiger, Tiger." In a plot that predated *Love Story,* guest star Yvette Mimieux (who won an Emmy) played the epileptic with whom Kildare fell in love. When she died, America wept for the lost young lovers. At the same time, MGM saw dollar signs, reuniting Mimieux and Chamberlain for the feature film *Joy in the Morning* (1965).

To everyone's surprise, the movie was anything but a joy at the box office. It was by no means a great movie, but it wasn't bad, either. Chamberlain and Mimieux were supported by an able cast that included Arthur Kennedy and Oscar Homolka. The story, based on a novel by Betty Smith (who had written *A Tree Grows in Brooklyn*), was about a poor law student and his wife. By the time the movie was released, though, *Kildare*'s programming schedule had changed from one hour per week to two half hours per week. The net effect of that change was that people were even less likely to plunk down the cost of a movie ticket when Chamberlain was available to them twice as often as in the past.

Of course, Chamberlain's track record as a movie star was already somewhat tainted. MGM had rushed him into his first starring vehicle in 1963 during his hiatus from *Kildare* with moderate box office results but poor critical reaction. The film was called *Twilight of Honor* and it was merely a legal version of *Dr. Kildare*. Chamberlain played a young lawyer with an old mentor much like Raymond Massey except Claude Rains played the part. It was even directed by Boris Sagal who shot the *Kildare* pilot episode. But the magic of the original pairing of director and star was not to be repeated. As one critic wrote, "Richard Chamberlain would be wise, at this point, anyway, to stick with his stethoscope." That same critic went on to say, "You'd swear he was actually afraid of the role."

The film had a curious cast of old and new actors. In addition to Claude Rains in one of his last film appearances, the movie also featured the redoubtable Pat Buttram, who had played Gene Autry's sidekick for fifteen years. Among the younger set, *Twilight of Honor* marked the film debut of Joey Heatherton, and it featured Joan Blackman as Chamberlain's love interest. It was Nick Adams, however, who stole the show, ending up with an Oscar nomination for Best Supporting Actor in an otherwise thoroughly forgettable movie.

Even though his role as a young, crusading attorney was strikingly similar to his Kildare role, Chamberlain had already been trapped by his TV image. "I received a letter after . . . *Twilight of Honor,*" he said, "from a woman who complained about me being in a picture that she couldn't take her daughter to see. See what I mean? I'm typed."

Chamberlain's lack of feature film success during the *Kildare* years represented his only professional setback. Movie stardom on a grand scale would always elude him, but the real surprise of that era was his sudden emergence as a top-selling recording artist. His fame as a singer didn't last very long, but unlike his experiences with *Twilight of Honor* and *Joy in the Morning,* the music business treated him very well.

Chamberlain's light baritone voice was first put on public display on March 19, 1962. He sang and danced on the *Arthur Freed's Hollywood Melody* program on NBC. He appeared along with Nanette Fabray, Shirley Jones, Howard Keel, Juliet Prowse, and Yvette Mimieux (the first of their many early associations). His singing debut was also his first TV guest appearance outside the *Dr. Kildare* series.

When an actor receives twelve thousand letters every month and he can sing, the most obvious thing to do is to put that actor in front of a microphone. And that's exactly what MGM did. His first single was a ballad adapted from the lovely and haunting song known as "The Theme from Dr. Kildare." It had been written by Jerrald Goldsmith who, along with Pete Rugolo, then set about to make the adaptation, abetted by Hal Winn who provided the lyrics. The song hit the record stores and the radio airwaves as "Three Stars Will Shine Tonight." On the flip side was "A Kiss to Build a Dream

On." The single became a major hit despite the fact that the lyrics were rather muddled.

Over the next couple of years Chamberlain released two albums and more than a handful of singles, most notably "Love Me Tender," the old Elvis hit. His first album, *Richard Chamberlain Sings* (1963), climbed as high as number four on the pop charts. His second album, simply titled *Richard Chamberlain,* was a more moderate success.

As befitting the role of a new vocal star, he made guest appearances on the Andy Williams, Bob Hope, Perry Como, and Dinah Shore variety shows.

Chamberlain was far more limited as a singer than he ever was as an actor. While his voice was genuinely pleasant, he rarely projected much personality in his songs. He was best at the ballads, such as "Three Stars," "Love Me Tender," "Rome Will Never Leave You" (an early Burt Bacharach tune) and "Joy in the Morning" (yes, he recorded that, too), but he was embarrassing in tunes such as "Blue Guitar" which sounded like elevator music, and "They Long to be Close to You" sung with technique but without feeling.

Chamberlain always wanted to be a singer. Early in his career he talked about his desire to perform in nightclubs. It was certainly natural for him to want to combine his acting and singing skills, but his efforts to do so during the rest of his career would meet with extremely uneven results. In fact, his first important attempt to meld those skills nearly sunk him clear out of show business.

8

ELUSIVE LOVER

*U*nlike some actors who have been destroyed by instant fame, Chamberlain reveled in his stardom without being consumed by it. As for his sudden popularity, he once candidly admitted, "I love it. I was such a hermit as a kid, it's wonderful." Yet, the irony is that he has remained something of a hermit despite his success.

It was natural for a strikingly handsome young man who suddenly achieved stardom and a modicum of fortune to find himself beseiged by women. It was just as natural for him to mistrust all of this newfound attention as insincere. That's why Chamberlain preferred people from the era he called B.K. (Before Kildare). For instance, he had become a close personal friend of Carol Burnett (B.K.) and they got along famously. In the first flush of his success, he said, she's "a remarkable, warm, sincere . . . and very talented girl who makes the wildest spaghetti in the world. I love her!"

Unfortunately, Carol Burnett (meaning no harm) referred

to Chamberlain's image as "squeaky clean"—a phrase that would haunt him throughout the early to mid-1960s. Others said much the same thing, but it was her quote that stuck. Nonetheless, they remained good friends because, after all, they had formed their bonds B.K.

The public, however, wasn't interested in Chamberlain's friends, they were interested in his lovers. He was America's number-one bachelor and every mother's daughter (and plenty of the mothers) would have killed for a chance to win the heart of the Prince of TV. It was not to be. He had met a young woman (B.K.) named Clara Ray, dating her for quite some time after *Kildare* was on the air. "I met her in singing classes," he said. "Something good did come out of those lessons," he added.

Chamberlain, under contract to MGM, had to play the publicity game, and that meant submitting to an interview with the powerful gossip columnist Louella Parsons. She asked him about Clara Ray in 1962. Chamberlain's obsequious reply suggests both the innocence of the early 1960s and his real station in the Hollywood hierarchy. He said, "I have had one girl for a long time, a young singer, Clara Ray. She went on tour with Marie Wilson. She is pretty, sings beautifully and, well, she's the nicest girl I have ever known."

It makes you want to throw up.

Douglas Benton recalled Chamberlain's relationship with Clara Ray, saying, "She was around [the *Kildare* set] a lot. I used to see quite a bit of her." Benton paused for a moment and reflected, "The women that he ran around with were generally intelligent; they weren't physically flashy. His mother was extremely strong and quite, quite bright. . . . It seems that when men grow up with dominant mothers they always gravitate toward intelligent women."

Many years later, long after *Kildare* was over and after scores of supposed liaisons with other women, Chamberlain was asked about Clara Ray. "She's disappeared into the great world now," he said, clearly having lost track of her. "The last I heard she was doing concerts in Rangoon, Timbuktu, places like that."

In fairness to Chamberlain, he always made a point of saying that there wasn't anything serious about his relationship with Clara Ray. He said the same about the many other women he dated. And there were plenty of them.

He was seen about town during the *Kildare* era with actress Linda Evans. She would later appear in *The Big Valley* TV series and then star on the prime-time soap, *Dynasty,* but then she was simply a young and beautiful actress in need of publicity.

"They were both starlets at MGM," explained Benton, "and it was just a buildup. I'm sure he took her to a lot of studio functions and things, but I know Linda," he said with a dry laugh, "and I don't think that's the kind of girl that really attracted him."

He also dated actress Suzanne Pleshette, who had guest-starred on *Kildare* in the highly regarded "The Shining Image" episode. Besides her movie career, she later costarred in *The Bob Newhart Show* during the 1970s. Unlike Linda Evans, Pleshette was very much the kind of girl that attracted Chamberlain. She was smart, forceful, and funny.

And of Chamberlain, Pleshette said, "He has a quiet, strong quality. And he also happens to be a lovely boy. He's sweet without being weak. He's not in the least impressed with himself. He's pretty, yes, but there's a good deal of dignity and authority which breaks through."

But not love.

Again, it was nothing serious.

In the case of his reputed dalliance with Yvette Mimieux, it was really nothing more than circumstance and a certain wish-fulfillment on the part of the Hollywood press. From their appearance on the same Arthur Freed variety show, to the famous "Tiger, Tiger" *Kildare* episode, and then to their starring together in *Joy in the Morning,* the two actors seemed as if they were the ideal couple. It just so happened, though, that Mimieux was married, and when she and Chamberlain were spotted dining together during the making of their feature film it caused a mild scandal. The reason for that, strangely enough, was that Chamberlain was so closely linked to his character of Kildare that it seemed outrageous for the pure and noble doctor to be spending an evening out with a married lady.

Chamberlain avoided similar problems with actress Dina Merrill, who was married for a very long time to actor Cliff Robertson. "I played Massey's daughter who never wanted to have any children and finds herself pregnant," recalled the actress. "It was fun to do. It was one of my favorite things that I've ever done and I really loved working with Richard. He's one of the nicest people; we've been friends ever since." She's not just saying that as most people do. They really have been friends for nearly three decades now. In a recent conversation, she said, "He called me and asked me to go to the theater with him and we had a wonderful evening. Then I saw him in California a little bit when I was doing *On Your Toes,* and this fall I went to see him in *Blithe Spirit* twice and we had dinner together. We had great fun . . . I was hoping to get him to come out to the country for the weekend . . . I'm going to take him to the O'Neill sometime at Waterford, Connecticut. He's dying to go up there to see where the new plays get born."

If Yvette Mimieux seemed like a perfect match for the young Richard Chamberlain, then Dina Merrill seems the perfect match for the mature version of that "dedicated kid" she "first met . . . on the set [of *Kildare*]."

Except Chamberlain and Merrill are just good friends.

Someone who knows Chamberlain well and who chose not to have his name mentioned said of the actor, "He's one of the most complicated people I have ever known. No matter how close you get to him, you never really know him. He's like an iceberg—seven-eighths of him nobody ever sees."

There are cracks in the iceberg, though, and if you look carefully you can peer inside. Or sometimes, when there are no apparent cracks, the ice can become so sheer it seems like a wall of glass, and you can look inside at the soul beneath the surface.

For instance, when discussing Julie Christie whom he once worked with in *Petulia* (1968), he gave a rare glimpse into his romantic heart. At first, he talked about her unique appeal, but then he ever so briefly touched upon his own need. He began by saying, "I wouldn't mind doing a nice love story with Julie. On or off the screen. Oh God, she's a fascinating woman. So elusive. She's like a wild horse, a wild mare running through forests. She seems untamable, uncapturable. Something very wild about her . . . Oh, boy, the way she looked at Warren Beatty at the end of *Heaven Can Wait* . . . If anybody ever looks at me like that, it's gonna be the . . . yeah, well . . ." He could not allow himself to say any more.

A friend who knew him during the 1960s and early 1970s said, "Richard has no private life. He has never loved anyone but himself. His entire life has been dedicated to proving to everybody he can act with the best of them, and everything that interferes with that goal is eliminated. He started out like a million other pretty faces in TV, and he achieved the unobtainable. He played *Hamlet*. Now he doesn't know where he's going as an actor, but he's just beginning to blossom as a man."

During that early blossoming period after *Hamlet*, in the early to mid 1970s, Chamberlain quietly dated Joanna Ray, the ex-wife of actor Aldo Ray. At another point, when he made *The Count of Monte Cristo* for TV, he met Taryn Power, the young and beautiful daughter of actor Tyrone Power. She was twenty-one and he was thirty-eight.

"I was lost and lonely when I got to Rome," Chamberlain was quoted as saying. Apparently, he wasn't lonely for very long after he met Taryn. "There was instant electricity," he said. "We love being together. I love her—that's all I can say." It was hardly a one-sided affair. The actress said, "After an unhappy romance a few months ago, I decided I would not get involved again romantically until I was twenty-five. But Richard has swept me off my feet. He's a wonderful, witty, and exciting guy."

He was also a guy whose career came before personal relationships. Taryn Power and Chamberlain were a short-lived item.

Chamberlain's tentative attempts to give of himself in love during these years sometimes left him bitter. "What keeps getting me," he once said, "is that nothing is like it's supposed to be. The entertainment industry did a great disservice to everyone with happy endings, great loves, and grand finales. Nothing lasts more than two minutes in real life."

Eventually, he became involved with actress Dixie Carter, whom he met while starring in the play, *Fathers and Sons*. Chamberlain explained their mutual appeal by saying, "It all boils down to warm and cool. Cary Grant is cool, Ingrid Bergman is warm, so they were electrifying together. I had that with Dixie. She's warm—she's a real woman."

Carter agreed that on the surface Chamberlain doesn't appear to be "warm." She said, "Richard doesn't give himself easily in life, but when he does he's irresistible. He has a raucous, earthy sense of humor that's devastating—it doesn't exactly match his patrician good looks."

He was dating Dixie Carter as late as 1980, and his close relationship with her at the time prompted him to say, "I think marriage is an experience I might have before too long." And then he hedged, by adding, "Or might not." Perhaps it wasn't marriage that he really wanted, but children. He wondered aloud, "What's it like having a little human that looks like you, who is part of your own evolution? I've had to do a lot of growing up before I could have the kind of marriage I would like to have, and before I felt I could have anything to offer children," he said. "I don't want to have, by accident, noisy things around the house that have to be fed—maybe you like them and maybe you don't. But I'm getting to the point where I can imagine myself coping with kids on a daily basis. Having kids takes your mind off yourself."

Chamberlain has always been enamored of children. When he was still a young man he admitted, "I don't think I'm ready to be married yet, but I certainly would enjoy children. I play with my brother's kids all the time. It's beautiful."

He wasn't saying that just for public consumption. He really felt that way. There is hardly a better example of Chamberlain's affection for children than the story Douglas Benton tells about the time the actor came to his house for a meeting during the popular peak of the *Dr. Kildare* series.

"At three o'clock [on a Sunday afternoon] he showed up," began Benton. "I sent all of my kids to the movies; I didn't want them to bother him. . . . We talked for about twenty minutes. Then I walked him to the front door and then went back to my office. About an hour later I wondered what had happened to my children; I had expected them back by then. So I went to the front door. We had a rather large lawn, and the lawn was absolutely covered with children between the ages of three to six or seven. And Dick was sitting in the middle of this crowd. It was strange—all the mothers were standing on the sidewalk on the other side of the street. He had been out there entertaining those kids for an hour. Obviously, they all adored him. When he finally got up and started to go, he walked up to his car and two or three of them were hanging on his legs and arms. He had a hell of a time getting away from there. But here he is, the hottest thing in television, and he takes an hour just to sit on the lawn and talk to these three- and five-year-olds."

It seems clear that Chamberlain always had a yearning for children. Unfortunately, he never had a strong enough yearning for any particular woman with whom he could have them. Recently, he sadly conceded that he had given up on the idea of having any kids of his own. And without children, he didn't see the point of getting married.

"There's something about the way life is accelerating," theorized Chamberlain, "that maybe people don't need long-term relationships any more—they can learn as much as they can from a person in three or four years. There's nothing that says a relationship has to go on forever to be worth something." He went on to say, "The relationships you make on a film set or in a play can be very close, but they're not permanent. We're so conditioned to want to hang on to everything. People are so in love, then they fight and hate each other. But the end of a relationship doesn't nullify everything that happened before."

Chamberlain has done his best to come to terms with his vagabond actor's life. It has been a lonely existence without any lasting love relationships. It would seem, however, that he has found enough love in his work to sustain himself.

9

"YOU'RE A STAR, AND YOU DON'T KNOW HOW TO ACT"

One day during the 1961–62 TV season, Raymond Massey had the highly respected British actor Sir Cedric Hardwicke as a house guest. Massey then invited Chamberlain over to meet the esteemed actor. In the course of their conversation, Hardwicke told the younger man, "You're doing it all backwards. You're a star, and you don't know how to act."

Chamberlain knew it was true. But he resolved that he would learn how to act and he used *Kildare* not as a springboard to riches, but instead as a springboard to learning his craft. Except after three years Chamberlain felt that he had learned just about all he could within the restraints of a weekly TV series.

"Perhaps the most dangerous aspect of being in a series for a long time is that you get a sort of acting shorthand, develop tricks for expressing the emotions instead of feeling them inside," he explained. "It becomes a waste of time acting in anything but close-up, because that's all the TV cares about.

You wind up acting from the neck up. The rest of you might be in plaster."

There were other complaints.

"The most boring part I can think of is the pure-minded leading man. He has no problems, no faults, no weaknesses. It's the frail man, the man with the mean streak, the man who is troubled and anxious who brings out the best in an actor. So I was coasting along, and couldn't learn any more."

Chamberlain wanted out but he was still under contract to MGM. When the ratings began to falter during the fourth year, Norman Felton, the show's executive producer, tried a novel approach to save the series. "In the fifth year, as an experiment, we let stories run as long as the demands of the drama would take them. We did it as a half hour twice a week. The first was four half hours. The next one was seven half hours." While the experiment failed, it introduced Chamberlain to the seminal concept of the miniseries, a new form of TV programming in which he would later become *the* dominant actor.

His miniseries success, however, was a long way off. When the last *Dr. Kildare* episode was aired on August 30, 1966, Chamberlain was set adrift. It was a crucial time for him. Important decisions had to be made over the next few years that would affect the rest of his professional life.

"After *Kildare* I felt I had to sort myself out; come to terms with what I wanted to accomplish in life," said Chamberlain. "I was hopelessly typecast, and I had to shake that." He also had to shake the Kildare persona living inside of him. "I was still behaving like him [for six months after the end]," he admitted. "After all, it's a great stretch of time to pretend to be another person. Shaking him off is like forgetting a love affair; the memory lingers on when the girl has gone."

The aftershocks of leaving *Dr. Kildare* behind were many. From an emotional standpoint, Chamberlain "went into the bends with insecurity." He also felt a chasm between himself and his peers. "After the series ended," he said, "I felt a slight resentment because the feeling was, somehow, that I had killed *Kildare* in order to do other things." Soon, he realized, that he had very limited options.

His two starring film vehicles hadn't lit any fires under Hollywood producers, so the movie-star route was essentially closed to him. And with his seemingly unshakable image as Kildare, TV didn't offer him much hope either. At least not in 1966.

That left the theater.

Chamberlain wisely continued to learn his craft in out-of-the-way places where critics could do him no damage. During the next year he began appearing in small stock company productions of well-known plays. He starred in *The Philadelphia Story* at the Royal Poinciania Playhouse in Palm Beach, Florida in 1966, then "attempted, abortively, to be Noël Coward" in *Private Lives* with the John Kenley Players who toured Warren, Dayton, and Columbus, Ohio in 1966. He also took a shot at the same play at Melodyland in Berkeley, California, before he continued to stretch himself, taking on the singing and dancing role of Tony in *West Side Story* for one week at the Westbury Music Fair in Long Island, New York.

It was all in preparation for his Broadway debut. He had signed on to star with Mary Tyler Moore in a musical version of Truman Capote's *Breakfast at Tiffany's*. The novel had been a hit, the film version of the story starring Audrey Hepburn and George Peppard had been a smash success, and there was every reason to believe that the Broadway version would be just as popular as its predecessors.

Famed impressario David Merrick was the producer, the original stage story (the "book") was written by Abe Burrows. The show tried-out in Boston and Philadelphia, for one month in each city. Everyone realized that the play just wasn't working. Chamberlain said, "The book wasn't right. So they started redrafting it, and adding to it, and subtracting from it. We perked up when we heard that Edward Albee would have a hand in it." The playwright who wrote *Who's Afraid of Virginia Woolf* rewrote the book. "But nothing could save it," said Chamberlain.

The show came to New York and went into previews. The official opening was several weeks away. An enormous amount of money had gone into the production and both Mary Tyler Moore and Chamberlain had a lot at stake in the play's success or failure. Both were TV stars (she from *The Dick Van Dyke Show*), and both wanted to make a name for themselves in the theater.

"The preview audiences had come expecting a lighthearted musical, and what they got was a tragic story with a few songs. So they laughed us off the stage," recalled Chamberlain. "The gypsies [dancers who travel from show to show] all knew it was going to close. I was so green I thought it was wonderful."

But Mary Tyler Moore knew the truth. "Mary would cry between scenes," said Chamberlain. "Up until then I had never known anything but miraculous success." His string of triumphs came to a screeching halt when *Breakfast at Tiffany's* closed after a mere four preview performances in New York.

"It flopped," said Chamberlain, "and the sound of the crash could have been heard in Texas. For me, it was like a death in the family. A tremendous disaster . . . Mary Tyler Moore gave a closing-night party at her place. We were all very manic—laughing a lot, drinking a lot. After the party, I walked by the theater; I wanted to see my name on that marquee one more time before they took it down. When I saw it, I started to cry, and I wept most of the night."

Chamberlain was of the opinion that a flop on Broadway wouldn't hurt his career. He said, "In Hollywood if you experiment and have a great personal failure, it's disastrous. People tear your page out of the address book. But in New York they realize that failure and success are both part of show business and ring you up to say they know how you feel." And he was right, up to a point. In fact, Cyril Ritchard wrote him a note after *Breakfast at Tiffany's* closed, saying, "Failure is such a large part of this business," and in the process reassuring the younger actor that better days would be ahead. But Chamberlain's failure on the Great White Way did affect his career, although not on the stage. People in the movie business, for one, were well aware of his sinking status. And though he didn't know it at the time, *Breakfast at Tiffany's* nearly sent him to the bottom of the thespian sea.

10

THE TURNING POINT

*R*ichard Lester, that iconoclastic director who burst upon the cinema scene with his rambunctious Beatle films, *A Hard's Day's Night* (1964) and *Help!* (1965), was the first among several individuals who helped save Richard Chamberlain's career.

The year was 1967, *Breakfast at Tiffany's* had recently drawn blood on Broadway, and Chamberlain was fading fast as a bankable star. Meanwhile, Richard Lester was preparing to film a serious, ambitious movie about relationships set in contemporary San Francisco. The film, *Petulia* (1968), was being made by an all-British crew but the financing was provided by Warner Bros. The first two of the three top leads had already been hired: George C. Scott and Julie Christie. Lester was still looking for his third lead, the man who would play Julie Christie's husband.

"Richard Chamberlain came to mind for that part immediately," said Lester. "It's not to say that we [Lester and screenwriter Lawrence B. Marcus] wrote it for him, but in the rewriting he kept coming to mind. . . . Physically, he was perfect. There is a line in the original script about a man who would try to sell someone a million-dollar yacht not wearing socks. There was that kind of West Coast American physical charm and presence."

Lester knew Chamberlain's work through the success of *Dr. Kildare* in England. The director hadn't seen many of the show's episodes, but he had seen enough to know that Chamberlain was worth pursuing.

That's where the problems began.

According to Lester, there was "extreme hesitation on the part of Warner Bros. and anyone concerned with the project, to be able to cast him . . . although he had that enormous success on television, he had only made two spin-off movies and I think at that time he had just failed in a Broadway show. So, first of all, I was told that the studio wouldn't have him at any price."

Lester paused and then slowly explained, "I was looking on this as being very much an independent production because we were using an English crew on location in San Francisco. So, I took a rather arrogant position and said, 'I'm going to have him.' Then, they said, 'If that's the case, he should be so grateful that he should do it for nothing.' I said, 'That's insulting beyond belief. If I think he's good enough to be the third lead in the film, he certainly deserves a proper fee. And what right have you to take an actor's dignity away from him?' It was that sort of chat." In the end, Lester had his way. "I cannot remember if he was correctly paid or slightly underpaid," said the director, "but . . . I was thrilled to be able to thwart the casting suggestions of the studio and win . . . because I think he was wonderful in the film."

Chamberlain was excited at the prospect of his role in *Petulia*. He saw his character as "a man who has been utterly destroyed by Julie, who married him as her ideal man and then pulls him down. So he becomes weak and vicious. It's everything that Kildare was not. I talked to Lester for two hours at Twickenham studios, and he gave me the part. I was delighted for two reasons. First, it meant that I could work with a director I admire—and any actor needs to work with an interesting and stimulating director to bring the best out of him. And, in any case, they usually have the best scripts. And, secondly, it would show another profile, and stretch me a little."

The filming went well. Chamberlain and Lester established a healthy working relationship and a good deal of respect for each other. The actor recalled, "Lester doesn't always tell you why he wants something, and you never know what camera is on you. He has seventeen cameras going all at once, taking long, medium, close-up, two-shots, everything. He gives you a sense of immediate importance; he takes each scene terribly seriously."

"I worked extremely happily with him," said Lester. "He understood and felt the character. . . . If he was worried about the part, he certainly didn't seem that way. . . . It was just a very professional operation—as all of Richard's work is. It was a film that went well in every way. It was a happy film as I remember it—as much as films can be pleasant to do."

Petulia garnered excellent reviews when it was released in 1968. It didn't do particularly well in the United States except at the art houses, but it did have good box office sales overseas. Richard Lester recalled, "It was the American entry into the Cannes Film Festival and had a broad European distribution."

The film's effects on Chamberlain's career were many. First, it stopped his slide into oblivion. Second, it gave him credibility as a serious actor in a highly regarded, successful movie. Third, it began the process of breaking him out of the Kildare mold. And, fourth—and most important—his association with this partially English production got him thinking about working in England.

*   *   *

"I had been in England once and I had liked it," said Chamberlain. "I felt at home and I got on very well with the people. I've always been attracted to skill and technique—not because I think you can ride entirely on that, because the English actors who do are boring beyond words. But you need technique to play the classics. So, I was attracted by that aspect of British training and by the simple fact that they have this level between amateur and professional theater—this rep acting which is marvelous. It's not your high-powered financial involvement. And I knew the BBC did a lot of dramatic stuff. So, I was thinking I'd go over and explore.

"Then I got an offer to appear on the Eamonn Andrews television show; he's something like Johnny Carson. I thought, 'Aha! It's an omen! They'll pay my way over! I'll pack my bags and go!' So, I went. Shortly after I got there my agent mentioned that the BBC was doing a television version of Henry James's *Portrait of a Lady* and asked if I would be interested in playing Ralph Touchett. I love James and love the novel."

Thanks to Eamonn Andrews's invitation, Chamberlain was in the right place at the right time. He took the lead role in the six-hour BBC miniseries. But as rehearsals for the production got underway, Chamberlain began to worry that his fellow thespians would look down their collective noses at him. "I was terrified about working with English actors," he admitted. "All that training and diction, you know. But then I found out that they were even more afraid about working with me."

Fame had its advantages, and professionalism was the key to his acceptance. He worked hard at the role of Ralph Touchett and he was rewarded with respect from his peers and accolades from the critics.

For Chamberlain, *Portrait of a Lady* (1968) was more than simply another early experience of playing in the miniseries format, it was the vehicle that finally opened up a whole new world of acting for him. *Petulia* may have stopped Chamberlain's downward slide, but his leading role in *Portrait* was instrumental in putting him on a path that would lead him not only to renewed stardom but to respectability as well.

Chamberlain has said: "That was the turning point in my career."

11

"YOU ARE HAMLET"

While Chamberlain was still just Dr. Kildare in America, in England he was forging a fresh identity. He was quickly cast in an all-star film directed by Bryan Forbes, *The Madwoman of Chaillot* (1969). The movie was largely shot in Nice, and it starred Katharine Hepburn, Charles Boyer, Danny Kaye, Dame Edith Evans, Giuletta Masina, Paul Henreid, John Gavin, Margaret Leighton, Yul Brynner, Donald Pleasence, and Oscar Homolka.

Hepburn had the title role, playing a woman who refuses to believe that life is anything less than wonderful. Chamberlain played her young, French lover. He was perfectly adequate in a movie that essentially wasted everyone's talents. Chamberlain conceded that the film "didn't work." Nonetheless, to be taken seriously enough as an actor to be included in such a stellar cast spoke volumes about his changing image. Had the movie been either a critical or a commercial success, it might have done more to help his career.

Chamberlain professed not to be unduly concerned. There was a method to his vehicle choices. When he played against type in *Petulia,* he said, "I took that role to show the critics I could play a villain as well as a good guy." When he joined the cast of *The Madwoman of Chaillot,* he did that "to show them I could do period roles as well as contemporary material, too."

When next he took on the most coveted role in the English theater, Hamlet, intending to play the Melancholy Dane in Shakespeare's own country, it seemed as if he wanted to show the critics that he had gone stark, raving mad. After all, no American had played Hamlet in England since John Barrymore had done it in 1929, forty years earlier. And even Barrymore had been savaged by the English press.

The wheels had begun turning during the BBC telecast of *Portrait of a Lady.* Chamberlain later learned that Peter Dews, the director of the Birmingham Repertory Company, and his wife, Ann, had watched the miniseries. During the show, "Peter turned to Ann and said, 'He could play Hamlet.' And she fell off the couch giggling."

Dews was undeterred by his wife's reaction.

Birmingham had but one repertory theater company, the one Peter Dews directed. Furthermore, Birmingham was not (and is not) the center of theater in England. It is, in fact, decidedly on the fringe. The city is better known for it industry than its arts. In the late 1960s they made cars and bicycles there, not Shakespearean stars. Dews was looking for an actor whose presence would sell tickets. And Chamberlain understood that. "They needed a personality for box-office reasons, and *Kildare* had been a big hit there," the actor explained. In addition, continued Chamberlain, "Peter wanted to be the Svengali who performed this miracle. He likes the idea of bringing things out of people that they didn't know were there."

It was certainly true that Chamberlain didn't know that Hamlet was lurking there inside of him. No one was more stunned by the invitation to star in the Shakespeare drama than was Chamberlain himself.

"When my London manager phoned me in Beverly Hills—I happened to be scrubbing the oak plank floors in my house—and said the Birmingham Rep wanted me for *Hamlet,* I dropped the phone. I felt pride, amazement, disbelief, terror."

Mostly terror.

"I felt as equipped to tackle *Hamlet* as a mountaineer facing Everest barefoot," he said. And no wonder. His entire experience playing Shakespeare consisted of five lines of *King Lear* during his freshman year at Pomona College.

His first reaction was, "This is impossible. I said no, my agents said no, and my friends just laughed." That, however, was not the end of it. The door had been left open by Dews and Chamberlain agonized over his decision. Ironically, his inability to make up his mind was decidedly Hamletlike. It was almost as if he were playing the role before he finally took it.

After he received the initial offer, Chamberlain said he was both "tremendously excited and very frightened. I wanted more than anything else to do it." So he called his mother for her opinion. He remembered: "Her advice was: 'There's no need to be frightened—you are Hamlet.' But she called back next day to say she didn't mean to imply I was crazy."

Dews had given Chamberlain time to reconsider and the actor did just that. "I studied the play . . . with everybody I could find in L.A.—speech teachers, drama teachers, friends. I lived that play for two months and got more and more in love with it and less and less sure that I could do it. Because I simply wasn't equipped technically to handle it. Or emotionally, as far as that goes. . . . I tried to decipher the role, worked on it here, and decided I just wasn't ready for it. Then one night I woke up in a cold sweat and I said to myself, you've got to do it." Underneath all the fear of playing the role was an even greater fear: "I thought I might never be asked again."

After his experience with *Petulia* and particularly with *Portrait of a Lady*, Chamberlain was beginning to have a touch more confidence in himself. One of his reasons for accepting the role was, as he put it, "I suspected secretly that maybe I'd come through in the end."

He knew what he was getting into. "You've got to be very realistic if you want to act Shakespeare," said Chamberlain. "You can't just hope. There are certain physical requirements. For instance, you can't mumble your way through. I had to relearn vowel sounds—Americans don't have as many as the English—and we are lazier about pronouncing our consonants.

"You've got to learn to act with your whole body," he continued. "As a TV actor, one has so many close-ups, that all I had learned to use were my eyes. Not everyone is prepared to go to the bother."

Chamberlain, however, was.

He had been hoping to land a role in the Mike Nichols film, *Catch-22,* but no offer materialized. As Chamberlain later conceded, "If I had done that, I would not have been available for *Hamlet,* which accomplished more for me, careerwise, than *Catch-22* would have."

With the movie offer dead in the water, there was no holding back on *Hamlet.* "I said yes, provided Peter would work with me for at least eight weeks before we went into rehearsal," Chamberlain explained. "He agreed, so I came to New York and we holed up at the Maurice Hotel—he was doing *Hadrian VII* at the time. Then I went back to England with him and his wife, and we worked daily in the neighbor's garage. We'd go over every morning and lock ourselves in and rant and rave and he'd scream at me and I'd carry on. Finally we began to get some results. Then we went into rehearsal."

There were other obstacles besides the difficulty of the role itself. From Chamberlain's point of view, "I felt it was like an English actor coming over to the states and trying to do *Abe Lincoln in Illinois* in Chicago." British Equity felt much the same way. "[They] didn't want me to do it. . . . I was accepted only after all the young British actors turned it down. . . . The British are very snobbish and protective about Shakespeare."

Money certainly wasn't the issue. Chamberlain did not receive great riches for his work. He was offered and accepted the equivalent of $110 per week for the chance to possibly make a fool of himself.

Once he was approved, Chamberlain realized that he wasn't the only one who risked getting egg on his face. "Everyone said that Peter Dews . . . was insane when he asked me to do *Hamlet*," the actor recalled. "And for the first three weeks of rehearsals, it was very depressing. I just sort of lumbered about the stage, whispering my lines, when what Peter really wanted was to have the walls come tumbling down in great bursts of emotion."

Early on, Dews told Chamberlain, "All you have to do is to find him, and play him, and get on with it." But the actor simply couldn't get a handle on the elusive Prince of Denmark. It was particularly embarrassing for Chamberlain because, as he put it, "I was surrounded by twenty-year-olds who came in and read like John Gielgud on the first day. On the second day, they had learned the entire play. I was still stumbling around onstage, not knowing where I was. I'm a slow worker. I can't give a performance until I know exactly what I'm doing and understand the part completely. But it had taken me three months to get up the courage to do *Hamlet,* and I was determined to go through with it.

"I was in a state of shock," he continued. "But amazingly enough, the company did not resent me. . . . If the other actors had been beastly, I'd have understood. They'd a right to be upset if someone without their experience came in and played such a role."

Chamberlain was relieved to discover that "there was none of that 'We're better than you' or 'We're doing you a favor letting you work here' stuff. In America, they would have eaten me alive. If I had suggested playing *Hamlet* in Hollywood, they'd have said, 'Who the hell do you think you are? Get back into your white doctor's coat.' But the British were helpful and kind."

They were also irreverent. Journalist Arturo Gonzalez, Jr., observed the rehearsals and wrote in a *Boston Globe* article, "Occasionally, the needle had to come out, and it was painful. In a dress rehearsal, as Hamlet's dead body was borne aloft, the musicians impishly broke into the *Kildare* show theme music, thereby convulsing the pallbearers and almost causing them to dump Richard unceremoniously on the boards. 'What could I do? I laughed too,' said Chamberlain."

There had been precious few laughs during the rehearsal period, though. In fact, just one week before *Hamlet* opened for its five-week run, Chamberlain was summoned by a distraught Dews. "He wanted to fire me," said Chamberlain. "I still couldn't speak much above a whisper. He was in despair. I told him I was sure things would come together during the run-throughs. At least, I hoped they would."

Chamberlain had thought that he would be somewhat protected from career-shattering publicity if he flopped, since he was performing *Hamlet* in Birmingham. He ruefully recalled that one of Dews's "prime selling points was that this wasn't London, nobody paid any attention to what happened in Birmingham, that we'd be reviewed only locally."

For good or ill, Chamberlain learned well before opening night that he was not going to perform in a critical vacuum after all. "During rehearsals," he recollected, "this girl from the *Manchester Guardian* was interviewing me, and she said, 'See you opening night.' I said, 'You're not reviewing?' She said, 'Of course. In fact, everybody's coming!'"

On opening night there was a feeling in the air of the French Revolution revisited, as a bloodthirsty crowd anticipated the downward descent of a critical guillotine. Chamberlain's presence in the cast did, indeed, help the box office of the Birmingham Rep, but a significant number of first-nighters were reviewers from all over England, and particularly London.

Chamberlain knew that his career was suddenly on the line. "The London critics came to kill me. I know that," he said. Yet Chamberlain had come a long way from his first rehearsals with Peter Dews when, as the actor later admitted, "I had no idea how to keep those soliloquies in the air, fencing, pulling that energy out of myself." But by opening night he felt that he had "probably solved more problems with Hamlet than any other role I've played."

He had also come to internalize the personality of his character. As his mother had said, he *was* Hamlet. And he further understood that "there's probably some Hamlet in everyone. Everyone who's thought twice about anything is Hamlet." And with the help of Peter Dews, the drama had crystallized in his mind around a single question. As he put it, "The central problem of the play is: What is action?"

He found out that night, when he went into action himself on the stage of the Birmingham Rep.

"I was frozen with fear," he recalled. "Why I got good reviews for the opening performance of *Hamlet* at Birmingham, I will never know."

The critic for *The Times* of London wrote, "Anyone who comes to this production prepared to scoff at the sight of a popular American television actor, Richard Chamberlain, playing Hamlet, will be in for a deep disappointment."

The *Telegraph* applauded, "A workmanlike and assured interpretation of the play with a graceful and intelligently spoken prince."

The *Manchester Guardian* joined in the chorus of praise, saying, "There are no gimmicks whatsoever—indeed, Mr. Chamberlain is attractively traditional in his playing."

And the *Daily Mail,* in a review headlined, GOOD NIGHT, SWEET DR. KILDARE, said, "Richard Chamberlain is a plucky actor and plays a plucky Hamlet. He earns his success. It is a straightforward, romantic *Hamlet.* . . . The perturbed spirit of Dr. Kildare may rest at last. In Mr. Chamberlain we have no mean actor."

Chamberlain's reaction to this surprising blizzard of praise from the critics was to say, "I was as astonished as they were." In general, he was rather sober about his success. "The critics didn't say it was a great *Hamlet,* but they did say, 'He can do it'. . . . They took me seriously, which was the most I could have asked for."

The astonishment of the American press was perhaps even greater than that of the English critics. Chamberlain's unexpected triumph was written up in newspapers all across the United States. Dr. Kildare playing *Hamlet* in England—and getting good reviews—was news. Never mind that the production was in Birmingham at a small repertory company. Chamberlain had succeeded where the great John Barrymore had failed. To his credit, however, Chamberlain continued to be modest about his accomplishment. When speaking of his good notices, he said, "They wouldn't have been good for Olivier, but they were good for me."

With his opening-night performance of *Hamlet,* Chamberlain walked through the door that had been opened by *Portrait of a Lady.* He had re-created himself as a serious classical actor.

After the reviews came in, he had the sweet pleasure of performing the play in front of a sell-out house. Each night was an adventure. "My Hamlet varied . . . because the character is hard to pin down. On some nights, there would be this dreadful three hours of silence from the audience, and I didn't know if they liked me or not. And then, at the end, there would be a great noise of applause. It was super . . ."

But perhaps the most emotionally rewarding moment of his Birmingham *Hamlet* came when his mother arrived in England to see him perform. After the play ended that night, she hurried backstage. Chamberlain said, "Her eyes were red and tears were still streaming down her cheeks. I said, 'Mother, you cried! I bet it was during the death scene, wasn't it?' 'No,' she said. 'It was during all that applause!'"

Chamberlain's stage *Hamlet* caused such a media sensation that he was asked to perform the play in a TV special. "Hallmark, my sponsor, got into TV twenty years ago [actually, it was eighteen years], and began its series of TV specials in 1953, with a two-hour *Hamlet* starring Maurice Evans," Chamberlain remarked at the time. "Now they want to take another look at the Melancholy Dane—with me. I'm the lead. It's wonderful, and quite frightening."

There was plenty to be frightened about. In the first place, in order to fit a nearly three-and-a-half hour play into a two-hour TV time slot, Shakespeare's text received radical surgery; the play's 3,800 lines were cut by more than half, down to 1,800 lines. That sort of editing would not please the more serious critics.

Even more daunting for Chamberlain, however, was the prospect of playing the lead in a remarkable English cast that featured Sir Michael Redgrave as Polonius and Sir John Gielgud as the ghost of Hamlet's father. In addition, the highly respected English actress Margaret Leighton played Hamlet's mother, Gertrude, while the talented Richard Johnson was Claudius. Only Ciaran Madden, making her debut as Ophelia, had less Shakespearean experience than the man in the title role.

"I was terrified when rehearsals began," said Chamberlain. "After all, Redgrave played Hamlet at the Old Vic in 1950. And Gielgud did Hamlet in 1929, six years before I was born, and he's done it five hundred times since. But I must say there was none of the stuff I feared, like those patient pointers from the master which begin, 'Well, yes, but what I did was . . .' None of that. Instead I got the occasional 'Richard, if I might make a suggestion' . . . but every time the suggestion was just right."

Egos were well restrained and Sir Michael was even over-heard to say of Chamberlain's performance, "He seems to have a very good idea of it."

The rehearsals were arduous and a great deal of care was taken in preparing *Hamlet* for the small screen. Chamberlain noted that an unusually large chunk of time was spent on the duel scenes. "You've got to get the timing perfect," he explained. "Hamlet can be all sorts of characters, but none of them can be clumsy with a sword. That's unthinkable."

In the course of drumming up interest in the show, Chamberlain tried to impress upon his prospective audience that his *Hamlet* would speak to them. "He's as modern as anything. Almost all of us are betrayed—if nothing else, betrayed by society. He is betrayed by the people who love him. Everybody does him in, except Horatio. Yes, even Ophelia."

Chamberlain's enthusiasm for his televised *Hamlet* caused him to write an article for *The New York Times,* in which he said, "My *Hamlet* is, I confess, against the prevailing fashion." Instead of "determined anti-heroes, rough figures slouching to their fate . . . our version is avowedly and unashamedly romantic, a revival of that earlier and longer-lived tradition . . . the prince as a Byronic hero."

Under Peter Wood's judicious direction, and intelligently

edited down to one hour and forty-eight minutes by John Barton, the Hallmark Hall of Fame production of *Hamlet* that aired on NBC in 1970 was a rousing artistic success. Swiftly paced and beautifully acted, the play became the most watched Shakespearean production of all time. Between its American and overseas showings and subsequent reruns, it has been seen by an audience well in excess of 50 million people.

Chamberlain was suddenly a hot property again. He could have done most anything he wanted in the early 1970s, which made his actual choices all the more surprising.

12

"A POTENTIAL NEW BARRYMORE"

Chamberlain had been given a complete set of Shakespeare's works by Peter Dews and the cast and crew of the Birmingham Repertory Company when he finished his run of *Hamlet*. It was a gift put to good use. One of the very first things he did between his stage *Hamlet* and his Hallmark *Hamlet* was to appear in a film version of Shakespeare's *Julius Caesar* (1970). As in *The Madwoman of Chaillot*, he joined an all-star cast; this one included John Gielgud (in the title role), Charlton Heston, Jason Robards, Jr., Richard Johnson, Robert Vaughn, Diana Rigg, and Christopher Lee. Chamberlain played Octavius.

Julius Caesar had been previously filmed by Joseph L. Mankiewicz with another all-star cast in 1953, led by Marlon Brando, James Mason, and John Gielgud. The newer Caesar came, was seen (by few), and didn't conquer. Even Chamberlain thought it was a bomb. "At the showing I went to," he said, "I was so bored that I left at the interval. A dreadful film."

The movie's failure, however, didn't hurt Chamberlain's newfound fame as a classical actor nor his star status. Simply being one among such a well-known cast had been an honor; in any event, his role had been modest enough that the film's poor reception could hardly be laid at his feet.

Meanwhile, Chamberlain continued to live and work almost exclusively in England. But his interest in the Bard had not abated and, by 1971, he was ready to make what he hoped would be his triumphant return to America in yet another Shakespearean drama, *Richard II*.

"One reason I wanted to do *Richard*," Chamberlain explained, "was that people don't know it well enough to have any preconceived notions about it. People would come up to me after the TV *Hamlet* and tell me that I'd given them exactly what they wanted in a certain scene; or exactly what they didn't want. In *Richard* most people don't know what they want, and the actor has more freedom to go out on his own."

He chose to make his return in *Richard II* with the Seattle Repertory Theater, with the much-admired Duncan Ross as his director. Again, he had chosen a smaller, less conspicuous locale for his serious theater work, hoping (perhaps) to stay out of the way of the heavy-hitter critics in New York. But if he hoped to avoid attention, his efforts were no more successful in America than they had been in England.

"I'm only just beginning to feel like an actor now," he told an interviewer during the run of *Richard II*. But if Chamberlain felt somewhat tentative, the critics did not. A local reviewer in Seattle, Dan Sullivan, was quite impressed. "It would be silly to call this a great *Richard*; but it is an astonishingly accomplished one," wrote Sullivan. "The accomplishments start on the surface, but happily do not end there. To begin with, Chamberlain has size. This has nothing to do with his actual stature, which is above average, but with the way he uses it." Finally, he concluded, "It is moving, it is interesting, it is Shakespeare, it is acting."

High praise, indeed, but nothing compared to the impact of *Time* magazine's glowing review. "For the first time in years," said *Time,* "a man capable of becoming a great and serious classical actor has appeared on the U.S. stage. Richard Chamberlain has a magnetic presence that holds an audience in thrall. . . . His delivery is intelligent, inflectively exact, and he conducts his voice as if it were an orchestra of verse. Chamberlain is inordinately handsome and bears himself with regal authority which makes him seem all the more a potential new Barrymore. . . . It is proof of Chamberlain's high emotive gift that members of an audience, so rapt that they never coughed, had cause, more than once, to wipe their eyes."

In 1961, Sir Cedric Hardwicke told Chamberlain he should learn how to act. By 1971, he was being compared to the legendary John Barrymore.

The actor was certainly pleased with the critical reaction to his *Richard II,* but he was particularly caught up in the work itself. Once again, he was performing for very little in relation to what he could command for a movie or TV role, and he told one disbelieving interviewer, "I would rather be a poor good actor than a rich bad one. Cross my heart."

After *Hamlet, Julius Caesar,* and *Richard II,* Chamberlain had to decide on his next project. Duncan Ross, his director at the Seattle Rep, had a very strong opinion on that question. "Whatever Chamberlain does next," he said, "I think he'd be very smart not to do anything by Shakespeare. If I know the American public, the very same people who said he couldn't do anything but *Kildare* a couple of years ago will start saying he can't do anything but Shakespeare."

Chamberlain did, in fact, intend to follow Ross's suggestion. And it was announced in August of 1971 that he would star as King Henry II in Jean Anouilh's Tony award–winning drama, *Becket,* at the Ahmanson Theater in Los Angeles in early 1972. When, later, a casting problem arose and no one of Chamberlain's stature could be found to play the title role of Becket, the play had to be dropped and another drama substituted in its place. Lo and behold, the new play was, yet again, Shakespeare's *Richard II,* done this time with an entirely different approach suggested by director Jonathan Miller.

The new *Richard II* was greeted with the same ecstatic praise the Seattle production had received. The *Los Angeles Times,* for example, declared, "Yesterday's dream date . . . has become a marvelous classical actor."

It was a proud return to his hometown, a place where he had grown up so unhappily, where he had found an empty, unfulfilling stardom on *Kildare,* a place he had left in search of himself as an actor. The critical reception could not have been warmer or more satisfying.

The production's success was such that plans were made to move the show to the Kennedy Center for the Performing Arts in Washington, D.C. In the nation's capital, just four hours south of Broadway, the reaction was still generally positive. The *Washington Post* said the production "heralded the rise of Richard Chamberlain as a classical actor of penetrating range." But Clive Barnes, then critic for *The New York Times,* had traveled down to D.C., and he was not bowled over. "He [Chamberlain] is certainly well-graced. He is good looking, with a light, flexible voice, and he moves well. But this was an exceedingly bland *Richard,* bland even in its insinuations and hysterics."

The good reviews gave Chamberlain the credibility he had always sought. The poor reviews were few and far enough between to do him little harm. And playing Shakespeare on the boards was an uncommonly exhilarating experience for him regardless of the critical reception. "Stage work is so rich, so real," he enthused. "To know right away that you're boring them, and then set to work to waking them up. I'm getting a little drunk on it all now."

He sobered up rather quickly, however, during the making of some of his nontheater projects during this same time period. The early 1970s were years of growth and change for him. Shakespeare was only a part of it. Surprisingly, after *Richard II* closed in Washington, Chamberlain never played Shakespeare again. Many years later he spoke of doing *Hamlet* once more because he felt he had learned so much and could add a great deal to his original performance. But no new production was ever mounted. And now he's getting too old to play the part. One expects, though, that someday—ten, twenty, or thirty years from now—he'll do as Sir Michael Redgrave and Sir John Gielgud have done and play either Polonius or the ghost of Hamlet's father in support of a new rising classical actor. For if Richard Chamberlain has become anything as an actor, he has become part of the classical tradition.

13

MEANWHILE, IN ENGLAND

From the late 1960s through 1971, Richard Chamberlain made his home in London, turning himself into an English actor. His speech changed and he spoke with a clipped, proper English accent, using language peppered with expressions that were far more appropriate for Picadilly Circus than Beverly Hills.

After *Portrait of a Lady, Hamlet,* and *Julius Caesar,* the projects he threw himself into during those years in England were eclectic and wildly adventurous. Working both in theater and in film, Chamberlain quickly amassed a small body of work that was stunning in its reach, if not in its breadth.

His most famous film from the English period is, without question, *The Music Lovers* (1971). This vividly visual movie about the life of the Russian composer Tchaikovsky (played by Chamberlain) boldly dealt with the musician's homosexuality and his torturous, unconsummated marriage to a passionate woman (played by Glenda Jackson). Ken Russell produced and directed the film, his first effort after his critical and popular successs *Women in Love* (1970). Glenda Jackson had starred in the earlier film, winning both a Best Actress Oscar and a New York Film Critic's Circle Award for her performance. Chamberlain was given top billing in *The Music Lovers,* however, despite the fact that the film was his first movie-starring assignment since *Joy in the Morning.*

There is a long tradition in the film industry of making biographical movies, but *The Music Lovers* was a breed apart. Then again, Ken Russell is not a typical director. Both compelling and repulsive, the movie's imagery was lavishly sensual, but incredibly self-indulgent. Scene after scene went on far too long, but the scenes themselves remained strangely unforgettable.

The Music Lovers received mixed-to-poor reviews upon its release, and it didn't do particularly well at the box office. Ken Russell received virtually all of the credit (from those who liked it) and the blame (from those who did not). Neither Chamberlain nor Jackson were much remarked upon except to say that they were often buried by the directorial histrionics. Poor notices or not, *The Music Lovers* went on to become a cult movie that consistently resurfaces in revival houses, film society showings, and on college campuses.

"To be asked to play Tchaikovsky was easily the biggest challenge of my career," Chamberlain told an interviewer in 1971. It was a challenge he felt ready to handle. "I would never have been able to do Tchaikovsky without *Hamlet* first," he explained. "The stretch into being able to play very intense material on a high emotional level was a breakthrough I made with *Hamlet.*"

According to Russell, he cast Chamberlain in the lead because "there was a certain quiet dignity about him which I felt the character needed. He was good to work with, very gentle and sweet; he did everything we asked him." But according to one report, Russell wanted him for the role because he was that rare actor who could play the piano well enough to fake the significant number of scenes that called for Tchaikovsky to be at the keyboard.

Chamberlain understood his casting to be simply that "Ken had seen *Portrait of a Lady* and thought I'd look good in the period, or something. And apparently he liked me." Chamberlain also understood that whatever the reason he was cast, *The Music Lovers* was a film that was going to get plenty of attention.

"Because *Tchaikovsky* [the original title] is such an unusual film, one doesn't know the effect it's going to have," he told an interviewer. "I wonder how it will turn out. I just don't know if I'm any good. It's fascinating—and terrifying—because Ken Russell is so brilliant and you worry about not matching up to his standards. It might be a great, great success and, if it is . . ." He let the thought drift away, no doubt wondering what effect the film might have on his career.

Given the way the movie was made, it was understandable that Chamberlain had no idea what his performance would look like on screen. "Ken creates before your eyes," the actor reported. "He's not one of those directors who thinks about it all in the study. You can watch his mind working. He used to sit there with a tape recorder playing Tchaikovsky's music and invent on the spot."

What Russell invented then had to be played. And the director didn't always know what he wanted until he saw it. "I never worked so hard in my life, weekends and the lot," said Chamberlain. "I was nearly dead with fatigue when we finished. I had no time off at all."

It wasn't just the work that irritated him. "The worst thing a director can do is bypass me as an actor, because I'm not so secure," Chamberlain complained. "Ken Russell moves you about like little figures in a maze, but everything comes out all right." Or at least he hoped so.

When *The Music Lovers* finally finished shooting, the actor felt defeated by the entire experience. It was such an ordeal for him that he actually said that he "was determined to give up acting. I've never been so depressed," he continued, "and it took me weeks and weeks to get over it. I love Ken and would do anything for him, but on a movie set he's so serious and demanding that he made Glenda Jackson and me do those scenes over and over, sometimes twenty times, until we couldn't move. It was no fun. That picture nearly put me in a loony bin." Yet, at the end of his grumbling, Chamberlain couldn't help adding: "But I loved the film."

Whatever one might say about *The Music Lovers,* it's a far better movie than his last, even more eccentric, film from his English era, *Lady Caroline Lamb* (1972). Written and directed by Robert Bolt, the movie concerns the short, scandalous romance between the wife of a famous British political figure and the renowned poet Lord Byron.

"Byron was like the first pop star," explained Chamberlain. "When *Childe Harold* hit England it was like the Beatles." Curiously, though, the movie was less about Byron than about the woman who fell in love with him, Lady Caroline, played by Sarah Miles. Chamberlain and Miles were joined by a cast replete with great English actors such as Jon Finch, John Mills, Margaret Leighton, Ralph Richardson, and Laurence Olivier. All of them were terribly wasted in a dreadful film that was hated as much by audiences as it was by critics.

Chamberlain consciously played Byron as an unlikable character. Unfortunately, what was lost in the harsh treatment of the poet was why Lady Caroline risked her reputation for him. Yes, Byron/Chamberlain was a beautiful man, but thoroughly lacking in charm. The best one English reviewer could say about Chamberlain was to say he was "physically startling—as if Aubrey Beardsley had supervised his dress, diet and decadence."

The most memorable aspect of the entire enterprise is, in fact, the way Richard Chamberlain looks in the movie. There can hardly be a more foppish appearance by a leading man anywhere in the cinema. The actor said at the time, "A few years ago, I would have been afraid to wear so much eye makeup in *Lady Caroline Lamb,* but Robert Bolt . . . convinced me it would be all right. Lord Byron was amazingly vain. He wore his hair in curlers, went on reducing kicks, ate potatoes and vinegar to whiten his complexion. I played him as a kind of mad genius, but with a kind of cheapness. I could only do that because I felt more secure as an actor."

It was commendable that Chamberlain felt secure in his talents, but he would have been better off if he had shown more talent in choosing his movie projects.

Happily, the prestigious Chichester Festival showed better taste in choosing its actors than Chamberlain exhibited in choosing *Lady Caroline Lamb,* for they invited him to star in Christopher Fry's brilliant verse play, *The Lady's Not for Burning.* Chamberlain was one of only a few Americans who have ever been asked to play there. Both the play and the actor were so enthusiastically received that the production, with Chamberlain recreating his role of Thomas Mendip, was eventually filmed in America and broadcast on PBS.

Joseph Hardy, who directed the TV version of *The Lady's Not for Burning,* was mindful that he was taking over a project that had already garnered its star considerable acclaim. Hardy conceded that Chamberlain "could have been nervous about my directing him in television, but he put himself in my hands and he never questioned the concept or the way it was shot."

The play (set in medieval times) is delightfully perverse. Hardy succinctly described the black comedy this way: "It's about a man who tries to get himself hanged because he's tired of life. He's a poet. And a woman is being chased by the townspeople because they think she's a witch. They want to kill her. He and the witchwoman fall in love and go off together in the end." The play bristled with an angry humor that cleverly teased and amused. The dialogue sparkled, in part, thanks to Chamberlain's mellifluous voice, which highlighted the musicality of the language.

The Lady's Not for Burning was a triumph both on the stage and on the small screen, the two media in which Chamberlain would continue to do his best work. With rare exceptions, this level of success would elude him in the movies. The fact that he has pursued his career in all three mediums during the last twenty years, though, is remarkable unto itself. It was England that gave him that opportunity. But it was in America that he ultimately brought his talents to their full fruition.

14

PANACHE

*A*fter *Lady Caroline Lamb* was sheared by the critics, Chamberlain was off the big screen for roughly two years. During that time, he continued his skein of biographical performances, begun in the movies with Tchaikovsky and Byron, transplanting his speciality to television with made-for-TV productions about the Duke of Windsor and F. Scott Fitzgerald. Both TV movies were decidedly ambitious undertakings, but neither of them lived up to expectations.

The first of these two hour specials, entitled *Portrait: The Woman I Love*, was broadcast on ABC December 17, 1972. It was based on the true story of Edward VIII's abdication of the English throne for the love of divorcée Wallis Warfield Simpson. Chamberlain played the king, and Faye Dunaway was cast as the woman for whom Edward gave up his kingdom.

The Duke and Duchess of Windsor were still alive when the movie was shot, and they were outraged that it was being made against their will. Edward died, however, before it was ever aired. He never saw any of it. In an effort to avoid offending the memory of the late king, *The Woman I Love* was banned in England.

"Actually, it's a very sympathetic portrait and had they seen it I personally think they would have approved," Chamberlain said, defending the TV movie. "But I was surprised to learn at the time that they had not been consulted on the project," he added. There were those who thought that the duke and duchess were miffed precisely because they were ignored.

"The studio took the view that the story of the abdication was in the public domain," explained Chamberlain. "It was a valid position, I suppose, but I personally was worried. As an actor, I can easily understand the value of privacy."

The actor wasn't entirely comfortable knowing that he was playing a man who didn't want any part of the production. "I didn't feel at ease with it until about the third day of shooting," he conceded. "I felt the real person's spirit was breathing down my neck. I had to be very careful, dignified, and very respectful. We could take no liberties. We worked straight from the biographies and news accounts."

Chamberlain lamented the two-week shooting schedule, saying, "Usually there's no rehearsal time at all so the first scenes are very tough. A lot of people have enough tricks or bejazz to tread water for awhile. But I can't. And it sure is uncomfortable to try to play scenes without knowing fully how you are coming across."

If he wasn't sure of his acting, he at least felt confident that he and Dunaway looked the parts. "We really managed to look very much like the couple without becoming plastic carbon copies," Chamberlain proudly announced. "Bags were added under my eyes, since the duke was forty-two when he abdicated, plus some rubber pieces were used, and my hair was changed to make the transformation. I found it helped, too, to have lived in England to have absorbed the attitude of the people toward the royal family."

In the end, though, the production failed because of its timidity. *The Woman I Love* stuck too close to the surface facts, never taking any chances in its interpretation of the events that led to Edward's historic denial of his destiny. After the movie aired, Chamberlain reluctantly admitted that he had "slid through" his performance. He might have more aptly said he'd slid *over* it, but he was not alone in feeling he hadn't done Edward justice. An ABC executive complained, "He brought nothing to the role."

But neither ABC nor Chamberlain were deterred from trying yet another biographical venture less than thirteen months later, when on January 6, 1974, ABC broadcast the DuPont Cavalcade of Television presentation of *F. Scott Fitzgerald and "The Last of the Belles,"* starring Chamberlain as the brilliant Jazz Age author and Blythe Danner as his wife Zelda.

The TV movie presented Scott and Zelda after their wild excesses of the 1920s, when they were struggling with the impending failure of their marriage. Eventually Scott sat down to write an autobiographical story called "The Last of the Belles," in an attempt to try to understand what had happened to their relationship. The movie then brought the fictional characters to life (played by David Huffman and Susan Sarandon) and the story continued to unfold on two tiers: in the reality of Scott and Zelda's lives as well as in the author's imagination.

Chamberlain had problems with the production from the start. "Quite frankly," he said, "I thought it was dangerous to do. It was a character study, a mood piece, and on television it was my belief viewers wanted more high drama. This was much more difficult to do because there is not a lot of plot."

In addition, the actor had trouble with his role. "He was a most elusive man who was hard to get a clear feeling about because he was so involved in his fantasy world." But it was more than that, finally, that stood in the way of a proper performance. It was the same problem that plagued him in *The Woman I Love*. "After I learned to act on stage," he realized, "I had to learn to act for film again. I discovered myself doing too much, too big. And I didn't notice it until I saw myself in the F. Scott Fitzgerald. While I was doing it, I felt like I was acting up a storm. But when I watched it, I felt like there was some reasonably interesting behavior, but nobody was home," Chamberlain said, tapping his head. "I was awful," he insisted. "I was so obsessed with trying to be like him that I forgot to make a person. I'll never do a recent historical figure again," he promised after the show received mixed reviews and a low Nielsen rating.

He kept his word for over a decade, eventually taking on the role of real-life hero Raoul Wallenberg and giving one of the greatest performances of his career.

While he was struggling with his TV movies, Chamberlain was also working in the theater. After his heralded *Richard II*, when he could have done almost anything he wanted on the stage, he surprised the theater world by choosing to star for five weeks in the charming but innocuous long-running musical *The Fantasticks*. It was his way of finally satisfying his urge to star in a musical after the disaster of *Breakfast at Tiffany's*.

At the Arlington Park Theater in Chicago, he played the role of the narrator, singing and dancing in front of seven hundred people every night beginning December 14, 1972. The choreographer of the production, Lee Theodore, said of Chamberlain's dancing abilities, "He can't make a bad move." And his sweet baritone voice was made to order for the gentle ballads of the play, particularly the evocative "Try to Remember."

David Lonn, managing director of the theater, gushed, "I really never thought Richard would take this role. How many distinguished people in the business would have any interest in coming to Chicago to do something new, to stretch themselves?"

Except it wasn't a stretch. Not after *Hamlet, The Lady's Not for Burning,* and *Richard II.* "I went back and did *The Fantasticks* just to see if I could do a musical," he said, "and now I don't think that's what I want to do. It was frivolous and not very rewarding, like eating too much dessert. I wasn't tired enough when it was all over. I like to be tired. Everything has built up to such a momentum, and I don't want to drop the ball. The next thing I do has to make me tired again."

After several unhappy projects during the early 1970s, he found exquisite exhaustion in his next theatrical project, Edmond Rostand's magnificent play, *Cyrano de Bergerac.* Produced at the Ahmanson Theater in Los Angeles with performances beginning in October 1983, Chamberlain's Cyrano was both a critical and box-office smash.

The well-known story concerns the unrequited love of an ugly, bulbous-nosed but brilliant cavalier (Cyrano) for the lovely Roxanne. The woman, however, is in love with all things beautiful and she falls for the handsome but vacuous Christian who relies on Cyrano to help make him seem witty and wise. It is Cyrano's words that win Roxanne's heart, but it is Christian who has her love. After Christian dies in battle, Roxanne flees to a convent, never knowing until the play's end that it was Cyrano all along whom she loved.

The play is one of the theater's grandest love stories, and it is full of irony, humor, and a fabulous spirit. Cyrano himself might say that the story has "panache." José Ferrer won an Oscar for his portrayal of Cyrano in a 1950 movie version of the play. It is an actor's vehicle, but only if the actor is up to the rich, demanding material.

Had he not been a star, Chamberlain would have been perfectly cast not as Cyrano, but as Christian. If ever there was an actor suited by appearance for the role of the beautiful young man with whom Roxanne falls in love, Richard Chamberlain is that actor.

Star clout aside, though, there was a far more compelling reason for Chamberlain to play the eloquent, heroic Cyrano instead of Christian. Joseph Hardy, the play's director, put it best when he said, "He is truly an exciting classical actor. He has the poise, the speech, the brio, to pull off those kinds of roles." He might have added that there are very few American actors who have those qualities.

Chamberlain worked closely with Hardy, and the director recalled that his star was "very hard on himself to make sure that he gets it right. He's very demanding of a director in that he needs to be directed, wants to be directed, and relies upon the director. The collaboration allows him to expand and make it better."

The more Chamberlain delved into the play, the more he found. "I was amazed by the complexity of Cyrano's character," he said. "He's so fascinating, and I got to like him so much. Chiefly, I liked his incredible life force, and his incredible capacity to love. And that insistence on living life on his own terms, that integrity." For a shy loner like Chamberlain, playing the title character was a special pleasure. "Cyrano was the ultimate extrovert," he said. "I could cut loose for the first time and play a character with no stops, just vitality and exuberance. . . . It was a great breakthrough."

It was a breakthrough for everyone concerned. "It was highly successful," reported Joseph Hardy. "In fact, it was sold out for every performance of the eight-week run. I consider it one of the best things I've ever done. And I think Richard does, too."

For the most part, the critics adored the show as well as Chamberlain's performance. In fact, his portrayal of Cyrano brought him the Los Angeles Critics' Circle Award. A re-

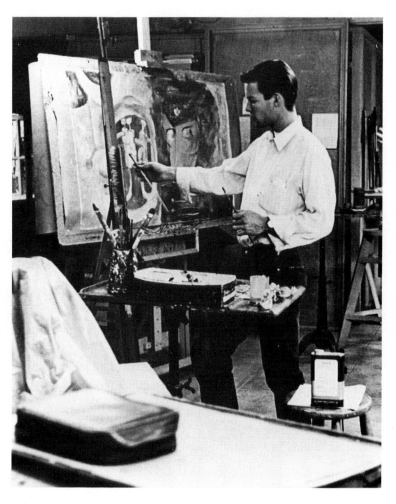

Before he became an actor, Chamberlain intended to pursue a career as a commercial artist. He is seen here in one of his college art classes. *Photo courtesy of Pomona College.*

A young Richard Chamberlain (third from the left) partying 1950s style. *Photo courtesy of the 1956* Metate, *the Pomona College yearbook.*

Chamberlain first showed an interest in the theater during college. While nobody at the time thought he was going to be a big star, nonetheless, even then, he looked splendid in period dress. *Photo courtesy of the 1956 Metate, the Pomona College yearbook.*

Chamberlain was rarely the star of his college productions. He didn't get serious about acting until his senior year. *Photo courtesy of the 1956 Metate, the Pomona College yearbook.*

Chamberlain, as Dr. Kildare, injected young teenage girls with panting desire. *Photo courtesy of* Movie Star News.

There is a dignity about Chamberlain no matter what his hairstyle, his costume, or his pose. He wasn't much of an actor in college, but photographs capture an image beyond his latent talent; they see the physical beauty and genuine sensitivity etched in his face. *Photo courtesy of the 1956* Metate, *the Pomona College yearbook.*

Chamberlain in between takes of his first starring role in the MGM movie, *Twilight of Honor.* He is seen here with one of his costars, an old Hollywood pro, Pat Buttram, who played the murder victim in the 1963 film. *Photo courtesy of Pat Buttram.*

Whether in period garb or modern dress, Chamberlain's appeal remains timeless. *Photo courtesy of* Movie Star News.

Although Richard Chamberlain and Toshiro Mifune didn't always agree on how to play their scenes together in *Shogun,* the two actors held one another in high esteem. *Photo courtesy of* Movie Star News.

Allan Quatermain and the Lost City of Gold, the 1987 sequel to the 1985 *King Solomon's Mines,* was filmed at the same time. Chamberlain, seen here with his costars Sharon Stone and James Earl Jones, seemed to enjoy making the films almost as much as the critics enjoyed tearing them apart. *Photo courtesy of* Movie Star News.

Chamberlain as John C. Fremont in the ambitious but flawed miniseries, *Dream West*. As always, the actor cut a heroic figure and turned in a richly textured performance. *Photo courtesy of* Movie Star News.

viewer from the *Christian Science Monitor* summed up the press reaction best when he wrote, "Mr. Chamberlain has an electricity on stage which his film and television appearances lack, and his rapport with his audience is immediate. He's a charming, dashing Cyrano. He has the style of the piece down perfectly. He knows how to throw away a comedy line and how to cast a flirtatious, conspiratorial eye at the audience. He knows how to move gracefully, whether he's fighting a duel or fluttering his fingers in self-mockery. He knows how to give a line a bitter edge without letting it turn to self-pity.

"His performance at the press preview was interrupted often by applause, and his bow was greeted by a cheering, standing ovation."

The show was faulted by some critics, though, as too bent on going for the humor rather than the heartstrings; they felt the production slighted the play's deeper values and that the ending therefore lacked an emotional punch. The *Los Angeles Times* critic in particular complained that Chamberlain's performance wasn't deeply felt enough. "I agreed with him," said Chamberlain. But that didn't change the actor's overall feeling about the production. He recently said, "The favorite thing I've ever done probably was *Cyrano* in Los Angeles . . . and *Wallenberg* was another favorite."

The worst thing about his eight weeks in *Cyrano de Bergerac* was that it ended far too soon. "I was in the dumps for about three months after [the run was over], and couldn't figure out why I was so depressed. Finally I realized that it was because I wasn't having that experience every night."

Cyrano had been the highlight of an otherwise dreary couple of years. Nineteen seventy-four, however, was the start of a whole new phase in Chamberlain's ever-changing career.

15

SWASHBUCKLER

*C*hamberlain had cut quite a figure as Cyrano, fencing his way across the Ahamanson Theater stage. Of course, he had also done his fair share of dueling in *Hamlet,* but it wasn't until he played Aramis, one of the Three Musketeers in the movie of the same name, that the actor established himself as an international swashbuckling hero.

From TV doctor, to classical actor, to dashing swordsman, Chamberlain became the 1970s heir to Douglas Fairbanks and Errol Flynn with a series of four successive films (two for movie theaters and two for American TV) in four years. Like *Cyrano de Bergerac,* all four films were period pieces set in France. *The Three Musketeers* (1974), *The Four Musketeers* (1975), *The Count of Monte Cristo* (1976), and *The Man in the Iron Mask* (1977) were all based on books written by Alexander Dumas. And it is to the Dumas-inspired storytelling that Chamberlain owes a debt of gratitude, because all four movie projects were critical and popular successes. The two theatrical films finally brought Chamberlain a modest measure of commercial success on the big screen, and the TV films became his stepping stones to miniseries stardom.

One of Chamberlain's best-known films happens to be a movie in which he has a relatively modest role. *The Three Musketeers* had an all-star cast which included Oliver Reed, Faye Dunaway, Raquel Welch, Christopher Lee, Michael York, Charlton Heston, Geraldine Chaplin, and Jean-Pierre Cassel.

The real star of the film was Michael York as D'Artagnan, but Chamberlain's Aramis, the most sophisticated of the Three Musketeers, was a pleasure to watch. No one looks better in period costume than he does. Wearing a hat with a massive white plume, Chamberlain was as dashing a figure as any whom Dumas might have conjured. And he put his fencing lessons and dueling experience from the stage to good use in this film. While Oliver Reed and Frank Finlay (the other two musketeers) were adequate in their swordfighting scenes, Chamberlain's ramrod-straight posture and noble countenance matched his deft thrusts and parries.

He was born and bred to play such roles. It was a shame, in fact, that he was so little used. "When I saw the movie," said Chamberlain good-naturedly, "I couldn't find myself." Nonetheless, the movie's international success was instrumental in helping to elevate his moribund reputation as a movie star.

The Three Musketeers was a rollicking, tongue-in-cheek telling of the old Dumas tale of the brash soldiers who were "one for all and all for one." Richard Lester, the film's director, had a wonderfully deft touch with the humor, handling the slapstick stunts with considerable aplomb. He also had a deft touch with his script. He had enough material to shoot two separate, complete films—which was exactly what he did.

The result was that the following year, *The Four Musketeers* appeared in movie theaters all over the world.

The further result was a flurry of lawsuits because none of the actors knew they were appearing in a second film. "Everybody was furious," recalled Chamberlain about *The Four Musketeers*. "It was very shrewd of Lester but that's why film contracts are so thick now—they've got to add clauses to cover that trick." Eventually, everything was settled between the producers and the actors. "All the stars agreed on a certain percentage paid in cash and another percentage of the profits," reported Chamberlain.

The Four Musketeers (subtitled *Milady's Revenge*) had a bit less comedy in it, but it was still a rousing good yarn, this one following the adventures of the three original musketeers plus D'Artagnan as they support their king in a power struggle against Charlton Heston (Cardinal Richelieu) and Faye Dunaway (Milady).

Richard Lester, who had directed Chamberlain in the contemporary drama *Petulia*, saw the heroic potential in the actor and wanted him for the role of Aramis in the *Musketeer* productions. On the issue of casting Chamberlain for *The Three* (and *Four*) *Musketeers*, Lester simply said, "He came to mind immediately." He went on to say, "The technique of filming those two films simultaneously meant that we had to juggle everybody's availability . . . It was a nightmare in that way, but fortunately Richard was available long enough to do that with us. Again, his physical abilities; that he rode well and that he had the ability to learn physical movement well [contributed to his casting]. Rehearsing the swordfights was all part of his skill. He is an easy man to work with. And I have enjoyed my time with him very much. He's a good, hardworking, serious actor who takes his job seriously. And he's also pleasant to have a meal with, so, what more can you ask?"

Chamberlain has always been a director's delight. He rarely gives one a hard time. But the *Musketeer* films were not always smooth-sailing productions. Chamberlain remembered that there had been a lot of consternation on the set because of Raquel Welch. She hadn't yet arrived, but serious problems were brewing.

"I know some people accused Raquel Welch of causing delays because she didn't like the costumes or the script, but I found her completely professional and quite friendly," said Chamberlain. "Apparently," he explained, "Richard had been a bit terse with her on the telephone long-distance about something, and she got angry and started causing a lot of contractual difficulties. And we didn't know that she had a perfect *right* to be peeved. It just sounded like she was being *incredibly* difficult. So we'd all decided not to like her when she arrived. We were all gonna give her the cold shoulder. . . . Well, she comes on the set in a kind of denim outfit, a shirt that's open way . . . you know, the buttons are bursting open, and all this skin . . . and her skin is like . . . like the surface of the most lovely gentle river. It's just beautiful, beautiful. And she was sweet, I mean, incredibly *sweet,* and all this beauty gushing out. And everybody just went, 'Ahhhhh. Okay, you're okay.' She was fun to work with," he added. "She was always on time, as opposed to some of the other people in the cast."

After having starred in plays, films, and TV movies, working in an ensemble with no long scenes of his own presented an actor's challenge. "The character I play sometimes has only one or two lines in one scene," he said, "and it's very difficult to establish a momentum. More concentration is needed."

Additional concentration on the part of TV executives helped parlay the dazzling success of Richard Lester's swashbucklers into a cottage industry. Alexander Dumas, they realized, could be mined for ratings gold, and who better to star in such costume dramas than one of the stars from the *Musketeer* movies?

Of all the major actors in *The Three* (and *Four*) *Musketeers*, only Richard Chamberlain had name value as a TV star. He had the added advantage of being considered a modestly successful draw as a movie star in Europe thanks to *Petulia, The Music Lovers,* and the *Musketeer* movies. These factors, coupled with his dashing new persona, made for a perfect match between actor and projects.

The famous Dumas story *The Count of Monte Cristo* had been previously filmed three times, the classic version having been made in 1934 with Robert Donat as the sword-wielding hero, Edmond Dantes. The remakes that followed were made in France, the first in 1954 and the second in 1961. The star of the latter *Monte Cristo* was Louis Jourdan, who played a supporting role in the Richard Chamberlain vehicle.

The story of *The Count of Monte Cristo* concerns a man (Edmond Dantes) who is imprisoned despite his innocence. When he finally escapes, he wreaks vengeance upon his enemies. "It's a great adventure story," said Chamberlain. "You know, I chose not to see the previous movie versions—I didn't want to copy even unconsciously. In the book, Monte Cristo has great second thoughts about the mayhem he's created in many people's lives and the innocent people he has hurt in destroying their husbands or fathers—the people who were trying to destroy him. He makes up for it, in part, by saving one of the innocent victim's lives, marrying her off to somebody else. In other words, seeding new love as a kind of penance for the killings.

"Well, we don't have any of that in our version," he explained. "Ours ends with a sense of loss and a kind of retribution through loss for his own cruelty and vengefulness. He goes to say to his true love, 'Let's try again. Let me come with you and help . . .' But she says, 'No, I must go off by myself,' and sails off into the distance."

The Chamberlain *Monte Cristo* was filmed in Italy, directed with style by David Greene (who directed *Godspell*), and it boasted a sterling cast that included the aforementioned Louis Jourdan, Trevor Howard, Donald Pleasence, and Tony Curtis as the archvillain Mondego. Taryn Power, the daughter of movie star Tyrone Power, played the young and beautiful love interest.

The real revelation for Chamberlain was Tony Curtis. "He's a brilliant comedian," he lauded. "And a good fencer—we have a duel to the death."

The production had been in a duel to the death, also, and it was almost mortally wounded. Happily, it survived, but not without some scars. Unfortunately, *The Count of Monte Cristo* was denied the opportunity of being Chamberlain's first hit miniseries. "The producer tried to sell it as a miniseries at first," the actor recalled. "After all, the book is 1,600 pages long and it's full of great stuff. But nobody would buy that so we condensed it into two hours."

It would have been impossible to do the story justice on a TV-movie budget, so a new marketing plan unfolded which allowed for a surprisingly lavish look for the film. In Europe, the movie was released to theaters and had a good commercial run. Shooting two slightly different versions—one for TV and one for theaters—was, in Chamberlain's words, "the only way you can afford to spend a million and a half for a TV film."

The actor was clearly pleased to be filming in Rome rather than in a Hollywood back lot—although he did find a few similarities between the two. "[Rome is] the most theatrical place I've ever been in. Everyone is an actor. When I go to the Piazza Navona I keep expecting to hear a heavenly voice say, 'Cut!'" The similarities didn't end there, either. Hollywood's modern gaudiness was matched by what remained of an earlier Rome. As Chamberlain said, "All this Bernini sculpture, all this Baroque architecture—they must have known it was funny. It's so excessive."

There was, however, one very important difference between the two cities, and it was the reason that Chamberlain particularly enjoyed his stay in Rome. "Here people meet your eye differently," he said. "In America there's a fear of admitting the sensual side of interest. Here it's so blatant and wonderfully sexual."

Memories of Chamberlain as the Duke of Windsor and F. Scott Fitzgerald were locked away in a dungeon when *The Count of Monte Cristo* was shown on American TV. Winning an Emmy nomination for his portrayal of Edmond Dantes, Chamberlain finally received a measure of respect from the medium that first made him famous.

That respect continued to grow when *Monte Cristo* was followed in 1977 with *The Man in the Iron Mask*. The Dumas story—once again dramatically shortened to TV movie length—told the imaginative story of Louis XIV of France and his twin brother, Philippe. Louis, a corrupt fop and puppet of the devious minister Fouquet, learns that his twin (and ever so slightly elder) brother is alive. Philippe is therefore the true King, so Louis and Fouquet have the innocent man (who has no idea who he is) sent to an island fortress where an iron mask is bolted closed around his head so that no one may see his face. Eventually, saved by Fouquet's enemies, Philippe manages to change places with Louis and he rules in his evil brother's place, hiding his own identity and remaining known to the world forever as Louis. As for the former king, he is sent to the fortress island and sealed in the iron mask for the rest of his life—a fitting retribution.

The story was turned into a Douglas Fairbanks silent movie called *The Iron Mask* in 1929. The famous remake starring Louis Hayward was made in 1939. Chamberlain had some big shoes to fill. And he did so, admirably. *The Man in the Iron Mask* was a hit with both TV critics and Nielsen households, firming up Chamberlain's reputation as a bankable TV personality as well solidifying his image as an actor who is always associated with first-class productions.

Like *Monte Cristo, The Man in the Iron Mask* had a distinguished cast that included Patrick McGoohan, Louis Jourdan, Sir Ralph Richardson, Vivien Merchant, Ian Holm, and Jenny Agutter. Also like *Monte Cristo,* the film was shot in Europe (principally in France), and given a theatrical release overseas.

Playing the roles of both Louis and Philippe, Chamberlain showed a dazzling range, portraying the evil brother as a mean-spirited, casually cruel man who is absorbed only by his own pleasures, and then portraying the good brother as confused and horrified as he is put in the iron mask for no reason he can discern, and eventually becoming a determined hero prepared to depose the king.

The actor's tour de force comes in the movie's climactic scenes when Philippe must pretend to be Louis. In other words, Chamberlain adds a hall-of-mirrors effect to his performance by playing a character who must act like another character, both of which are his own creations. And when Philippe, pretending to be Louis, meets his mother for the first time, the actor's face and voice tell a dozen stories of loss, regret, despair, and shock. The scene is charged with emotion, all of it coming from Chamberlain's restrained yet forceful playing.

As always, the tall, lean actor seemed ideally suited to the period costumes. The wigs, ruffles, feathers, etc. never looked silly on him. He even wore the poorly designed iron mask with a certain dignity. The mask would have made most actors look foolish. At one point, it got around that he wore the mask to lunch one day. He found that rumor amusing, and replied, "I never wore it to lunch. I did eat a little cheese through it but the mask was terribly claustrophobic."

When asked how it came to pass that he had become a swashbuckling hero in four Dumas films in four successive years, Chamberlain could only laugh and say, "I'm a cape freak."

These weren't the only movies he made during the mid-1970s. They are, in retrospect, however, his most important. From the mid-1970s until 1980, Chamberlain tried mightily to become a movie star in the fullest sense of that expression. "One part of me wants to be the biggest star in the business," he said. "Another part of me says, 'The hell with all that. The only important thing is to be a good actor.'"

During the latter half of the 1970s, his desire to be a star seemed to mostly outweigh his goal of being a good actor. Or, at the very least, the movie roles he was offered (and accepted) didn't give him much opportunity to excel at his craft. Still, his movies during this period, though a bizarre mishmash of projects, show, in their own peculiar way, a willingness to tackle new and different kinds of acting—including acting purely for money.

16

THE MOVIE STAR

*R*ichard Chamberlain may have appeared in a higher percentage of all-star films than any living actor. He continued in that tradition in 1974 when he landed a role in *The Towering Inferno,* which starred Paul Newman, Steve McQueen, William Holden, Fred Astaire, Faye Dunaway, Susan Blakely, Jennifer Jones, O. J. Simpson, Robert Vaughn, and Robert Wagner.

The movie told the tale of a brand-new skyscraper, the tallest building in the world at 136 stories. During the grand opening bash on the tower's rooftop, a fire breaks out in the building and all hell breaks loose until the two biggest stars in the film, Paul Newman and Steve McQueen, devise a method for putting out the blaze. But before that happens, a great many of the movie's characters die harrowing deaths. Chamberlain kiddingly said the film was "called 'Toast Your Favorite Star.'"

He was one of those who was toasted. "I play the electrical contractor on the world's tallest skyscraper," he said, explaining his role. "I've fudged on the wiring, and a fire breaks out. A lot of people die . . . me included. They tell me that audiences applaud when I get killed. That's great . . . I also drink a lot, cheat on my wife, and tell my father-in-law, Bill Holden, to go to hell. It's a delightful part . . . I'm really wicked—a more double-dyed villain you'll never see!" Later, he went on to say, "It was a fascinating acting challenge. I had to supply all the motivations and make the character make sense—and it worked."

The Towering Inferno was the apotheosis of the disaster film, killing and maiming its characters on a bigger budget than any other movie of its kind before or since the 1970s disaster film craze that began in earnest with *The Poseidon Adventure* (1972). The movie boasted the involvement of two major Hollywood studios, 20th Century–Fox and Warner Bros., both of whom owned rights to similar stories. Rather than compete with each other, they pooled their stories, their resources, and their stars to make a major hit movie. Irwin Allen, famous for being the master of the disaster epic, was the producer. John Guillermin directed the actors, while Allen directed the action/special-effects sequences.

After he had worked so hard to establish himself as a serious actor, it was something of a surprise to see Richard Chamberlain's name in the cast list. When asked what had motivated him to appear in the film, the actor replied, "I did that for several reasons. I thought it might be good to do a big commercial film like that. I was faintly"—he paused and reconsidered—"I was rather interested in the part," he said. "Everyone should work with Irwin Allen once. He's a real character."

At one point, before he was associated with *The Towering Inferno,* Chamberlain expressed an interest in breaking free of the classical-actor mold he had created for himself. He said, "I am anxious to get back into something that means something in terms of modern times. I want to play an American guy. I'm very curious to see what it feels like to do that again, because I haven't done it for so long. But I hope to continue in the classical stuff," he made a point of adding. "There's no reason why you can't do as much as your instrument and brain are capable of doing. It's very difficult, though, to keep from being stuck in some kind of bag. George C. Scott has managed to avoid it as well or better than anybody. It really makes me laugh when people wonder if I can play modern American people any more. 'Can you do American parts any more, Dick?' That's really dumb."

He certainly showed that he could play a sleazy American on the make, but it was a surprise that he chose such a lightweight entertainment in which to do it. Still, he made his point and, in the process, he enjoyed the unique experience of being part of a major Hollywood production.

"It was fun," he reported unself-consciously of his time on the set of *The Towering Inferno*. "It's so good to be in a moneymaker, a real old-fashioned U.S. movie, full of stars." Even to an actor who had performed alongside the likes of Sir Ralph Richardson, Sir John Gielgud, Louis Jourdan, Glenda Jackson, and Oliver Reed, to name just a few of his previous English and European costars, there was something special about joining a cast that boasted so many Hollywood legends. "Just being on the set of *The Towering Inferno* with the likes of Astaire and Holden and Newman and McQueen—what a gas!" he said with all the verve of a genuine movie fan.

"The thrill was meeting Fred Astaire," said Chamberlain, and who could disagree? "I was afraid to talk to [him] for the first few days on the set. I finally got up the nerve to go up and say, 'Hi, Mr. Astaire.' He was sweet, completely unpretentious. . . . He's exactly the way you'd imagine him—modest and shy, funny and interesting. And he manages to maneuver every conversation so that you're talking about yourself."

Fred Astaire and the other Hollywood stars aside, Chamberlain seemed somewhat defensive about his movie work. He complained to an interviewer, "People are always saying, 'You really prove yourself on the stage, don't you, because films are just bits and pieces?' But film is ten times harder than stage acting. Film acting is a matter of thinking and feeling the right thing. There's no way of fooling a camera, you just can't. It goes right through you.

"The difficulty with film—whether television or movies—is all the waiting around while they set up shots," he explained. "You can't read books or play games or do anything like that because you can't afford to get your mind that far out of the reality of the picture. You can't do anything but sit and wait and try to husband this energy and keep it going so that when they're finally ready for you, you're ready to do it and do it fast.

"Another difficulty with filmmaking," Chamberlain continued, warming to his subject, "is that you don't know when you're going to do any particular thing. In the theater, you know when you check in, when you put on your makeup, when you do your voice exercises; and then, from the beginning to end, you're the boss. In film, you're really the low man on the totem pole as an actor. When they're ready for you, they tell you—and they may change from one scene to another without warning. You may suddenly be doing a love scene with someone you've never met before! You rehearse it two or three times and then shoot, and you've really got to think fast to make it rich at all.

"It gets both easier and harder as you go along. A minimum level of performance gets easier, but your minimum level gets less and less satisfactory to you, so you raise your standards. You keep raising your standards, and it's a constant challenge."

By 1978, the challenge had seemingly worn him down. If,

as Chamberlain had said, every actor should work with Irwin Allen once, he had no such excuse when he worked with the producer again, lending his name to the box office dud, *The Swarm*. It was another all-star film, this one about killer bees. Chamberlain joined Michael Caine, Katharine Ross, Henry Fonda, Richard Widmark, Olivia de Havilland, Fred MacMurray, Ben Johnson, and José Ferrer in a movie that not only wasted its talented actors, it humiliated them.

Chamberlain's reason for making the film, however, was straightforwardly mercenary. He good-naturedly said that he made the movie "for money . . . I was paid $300,000 for a couple of weeks and it helped me buy a home in Hawaii."

This same actor who appeared in *The Towering Inferno* and *The Swarm*—which were the most obvious sort of Hollywood concoctions during the 1970s—also starred in two of the most eccentric movies of the decade, *The Slipper and the Rose* (1976) and *The Last Wave* (1978). And even those two movies were as different as two films can be.

The Slipper and the Rose was a musical version of the Cinderella story, with Chamberlain in the role of Prince Charming. It seemed on the surface to be a movie better suited to the 1950s than the mid-1970s. Who would take such a movie seriously? Even Chamberlain admitted that he thought making *The Slipper and the Rose* "would be a hoot." He decided to star in the movie anyway, "because I like Bryan [Forbes, the director] so much and also because I had never done a musical film before. It was my swan song to 'G' leads," he joked.

The movie was made in England, with Gemma Craven as Cinderella, and such stalwart English actors as Margaret Lockwood, Kenneth More, and Dame Edith Evans playing in support. The story of *The Slipper and the Rose* differed rather markedly from its fairy-tale source with respect to the prince. Whereas the original story is essentially about the poor girl who is abused by her stepmother and stepsisters, the movie gives more than equal weight to the young nobleman's search for a woman he can love. The movie's comic relief is also found at court, with amusing performances by the rest of the royal family.

The Slipper and the Rose opened at Radio City Music Hall for the Christmas season, receiving mixed reviews. Some critics laughed and sneered at it, but others found it refreshing and delightful. It was not a big box-office success, but it wasn't *The Swarm,* either.

Chamberlain gave (you'll excuse the pun) a charming performance as the prince. His singing was both sweet and vigorous, and his pleasing baritone was easy to take in a movie that was designed to be exactly that—easy to take. Even more impressive was his dancing. Chamberlain always moved well in his dashing Dumas roles, but here he danced with a natural grace that seemed royally effortless.

While he understood that "without the looks I wouldn't have got the part," looks weren't enough to carry him. The role, he discovered, was "so much more difficult because the material is less helpful." After all, who is Prince Charming if not a one-dimensional ideal? In any case, the actor was able to add some color and just a bit of depth to his character, helping to keep the whole enterprise afloat in between the musical numbers. Gemma Craven as Cinderella was less successful at holding up her end of the film. Her thin, reedy voice made Chamberlain's seem that much more commanding, but the movie suffered from a weak female lead whether she was singing or acting.

For all its foolishness, *The Slipper and the Rose* was one of the few Chamberlain non–all-star big-screen vehicles that was also a satisfying movie.

Another one of those rare good movies was *The Last Wave* (1978), directed by Australian Peter Weir. The film had a vague plot, but it was really a mood piece, offering sensual, disturbing, and symbolic imagery in the place of a story line. Chamberlain was the only name actor in the movie. His most memorable costars were the Australian outback and its aborigines.

The actor showed considerable courage in signing on to make a movie with a script that he later kindly described as "indeterminate." He got involved in the project because "I liked the director's work so much, it was worth a gamble." The amorphous plot concerned a modern-day lawyer (Chamberlain) taking on a case defending several aborigines who were accused of murder. Chamberlain's character was the window through which the audience learned about these primitive people. And it was quite an education, both for the actor and the audience.

"I got that sense, being with the aborigines," said Chamberlain, "that there were worlds of knowledge and connection that they knew about and felt that I didn't know anything about at all. . . . They say they know how to 'sing a man to death.' Sometimes they lose you in their thinking—an aborigine boy told me, 'When you walk alone at night on the beach, the moon takes you up and you meet the father . . .' Their connection with the earth was fascinating to me—partly because the film was about the way man has lost his connections with the planet, with space, with the moon, with his friends and family. We've become so isolated that it was time for this kind of great cleansing wave of nature to come and wipe us out and start over again."

The Last Wave seemed to settle something in Chamberlain's mind about his ultimate destination in his life and work. Perhaps it was just coincidental, but despite the critical praise for the movie and its moderate success as an art-house attraction, after *The Last Wave*, Chamberlain seemed to pull back from his quest to become a full-fledged movie star.

It was around the time that he agreed to make *The Last*

Wave that he told an interviewer, "I'm a 'moderately bankable' actor rather than a 'super colossally bankable' actor. I wouldn't mind being a movie star," he conceded, "but the price is so extraordinary in terms of what you dare to do. You stand to lose so much by being a 'star.' You get hooked on the extraordinary gamble—you can only do high-tension, high-pressure pictures—when you're in that position, doing a play in Seattle wouldn't cut the mustard."

In other words, the allure of the fame and glory that comes with movie stardom had begun to diminish. He had clearly become somewhat cynical about Hollywood, saying, "It seems to me there's a very definite hierarchy of money here. You have actors who get a million dollars a picture, actors who get two, and I've heard people say, 'He's just a $200,000-a-picture actor.' As if that wasn't a lot of money."

In the end, Chamberlain didn't want to be judged by his paycheck, but rather by his work. A friend named Hal Halverstadt once said of him, "He's smart. He's got a good sense of perspective. He's thoughtful. He's always analyzing situations. He's always evaluating himself." What Chamberlain undoubtedly saw when he considered his film career in the late 1970s was that he was going nowhere fast. Though he still had an eminently youthful appearance in 1978 after *The Swarm,* he was already well past forty and unlikely to become a matinee idol anytime soon. He would have also noticed that, his all-star films aside, his best as well as most popular work had been *The Count of Monte Cristo* and *The Man in the Iron Mask,* both made for TV.

Chamberlain didn't turn his back entirely on the silver screen after *The Swarm.* There were other movies that he wanted to make. He had been interested in *The French Lieutenant's Woman,* but Jeremy Irons got the part when it was finally made into a movie. Also, at one point he was supposed to star in the film adaptation of Erich Segal's *Man, Woman and*

Child, but he had to bow out because it interfered with the making of *The Thorn Birds.* He was lucky on that one; instead of one more flop in the movies, he ended up in one of the most loved miniseries in TV history.

Though he avoided the *Man, Woman and Child* fiasco, he still had his share of movie disappointments in the 1980s. But unlike the earlier decade, his focus had changed dramatically. During the last ten years he has mostly appeared either in the theater or on television, enhancing his reputation both as a serious actor and as an important TV star.

Chamberlain is fond of saying, "I've invented my own game. Television is supposed to be bad for your film career . . . theater is supposed to be a waste of time for someone with a film career . . . I go back and forth among all three." True enough, but his record as a film star is erratic and spotty, while his successes in theater and television are genuinely remarkable.

17

A PERSONAL QUEST

*I*n retrospect, it is no surprise that Chamberlain was drawn to the otherworldliness of Peter Weir's *The Last Wave*. The film's search for a connection to nature has mirrored his own quest for a personal sense of connection to the world.

Early in his career, Chamberlain looked for his self-worth solely in his work. In a moment of candor, he admitted, "After I got into acting I needed to make a name, to pin a plaque on myself—an accomplishment I could point to and say, 'That's me!'" But after becoming a great success, the chasm he felt in his soul had not been filled. "I still had this core of discomfort," he said. "I was so busy pleasing people that I lost touch with myself. I didn't know when I was angry; I'd get withdrawn. I inverted the anger and screwed myself up."

During the early 1970s Chamberlain went into analysis, later becoming involved with Gestalt therapy and experimenting with Rolfing. It seemed to help. "During my four years in analysis," he said, "I worked through my uptightness."

The real emotional breakthrough, however, came when Chamberlain discovered Dr. Brugh Joy, a former internist who left traditional medicine to become a holistic healer. "Back in the seventies," Chamberlain explained to Jim Jerome of *US* magazine, "I did seventeen-day workshops at his [Joy's] ranch in the Mojave Desert. By the end of the second week, I was so close to everybody, so completely trusting of them, that it blew my mind. I was two different people coming into and going out of that retreat. Instead of being formal and aloof, I now tend to get closer and more intimate with people who really interest me."

Chamberlain continued going on retreats with Dr. Joy well into the 1980s, many of them taking place at the doctor's Sky Hi Ranch in the Lucerne Valley desert of southern California. This was Shirley MacLaine territory, but the geography was mental, not topograpical. "Brugh can know you by your energy field and balance your energies out to the point that you feel incredibly wonderful," said Chamberlain. "I have much more positve and creative directions, a much better flow in my life, and my relationships are more fun and have more depth."

Even after Chamberlain stopped going on the retreats, he continued to take much of what Dr. Joy taught to heart. "You know, they talk about us using one-tenth of our brains," expounded the actor. "I think we use one-tenth of our whole being, or maybe one-fiftieth or one-one hundreth. We just don't know what potential we have in so many different directions. And if you can encounter instructors who can begin to open your eyes to some of the human qualities that you already possess but just don't know about, then your life is immeasurably enriched . . .

"Unfortunately," he continued, "the Puritan, Christian ethic is that our nature itself is corrupt, and I think that is a criminal misinterpretation. I think our basic nature is in fact divine. I think there's a seed of divinity in each of us, and that's what we need to tune to."

One of Chamberlain's friends had to concede that "sometimes he becomes so ethereal it seems as if he is on one wavelength and the rest of the world is on another." Another friend, however, once commented that "Dick really is whatever he thinks he is at the moment." But whatever one might make of Chamberlain's emotional changes, a third friend observed the most telling evidence of all: "He has a kind of inner calm that is unusual for a working actor."

If Chamberlain was looking for peace, it would seem that he had found it.

Dr. Joy, who was an early advocate of what is now called the New Age movement, wrote a memoir called *Joy's Way: A Map for the Transformational Journey,* and ever since Chamberlain used his teacher's map for his own personal journey, the actor has repeatedly tried to turn the doctor's book into a TV movie. It has been a pet project of his for a considerable number of years, often announced but never produced.

What was produced, however, was an eager, questioning mind. Chamberlain continued to search for inner truths. On the set of *The Thorn Birds,* the actor was often found in deep, philosophical discussions with the miniseries' religious consultant, Father Terrance Sweeney, who said of Chamberlain, "He seems to be on a personal quest. He has a very intense level of inquisitiveness. He wants to know the meaning of life. Who is God? How is God experienced? What is the meaning of relationships? How does his professional life affect his life as a human being?"

The search continued in the mid-1980s with Chamberlain's interest in channeling, bringing him within the sphere of J. Z. Knight, who claimed that when she was in a trance, a 35,000-year-old soldier from Atlantis named Ramtha spoke through her. Chamberlain wasn't alone in his fascination with Knight.

Shirley MacLaine, Linda Evans, and other Hollywood types were also drawn to the channel.

Chamberlain claims that during the last decade he has become a much happier person than he ever was in his youth or after his early success in the 1960s and much of the 1970s. Perhaps not coincidentally, his happiest years have also been, by and large, the years of his greatest, most memorable achievements.

18

THE PLAY'S
THE THING

*I*n the midst of his movie-star years in the mid-1970s, Chamberlain refused to fully abandon his stage career. In 1975, he had hoped to star for the first time on Broadway in a play based on James Kirkwood's novel, *P.S. Your Cat Is Dead*. When those plans fell through, he became involved in a Los Angeles revival of Tennessee Williams's classic drama, *The Night of the Iguana*.

The play had originally been a hit on Broadway, and later a top-grossing movie with Richard Burton in the leading role of T. Laurence Shannon, a defrocked priest working as a drunken tour guide in Mexico, tormented by his inner passions as he flames the sexual fires of several beautiful women. It was a rich and wonderful part for Chamberlain, and he was delighted to be reunited with director Joseph Hardy, who had previously worked with him on *Cyrano de Bergerac* in 1973 and the PBS version of *The Lady's Not for Burning* in 1974.

Coming into the new production of *Iguana*, Chamberlain was admittedly unsatisfied with the intensity of his past stage work. "I've been lousy lots of times," he said. "I've gotten away with it. They clapped and told me I was wonderful." This time, he didn't want to fool either the audience or himself.

"Nothing much happens in *Iguana* plotwise," explained Chamberlain, discussing the actor's challenge, "so it's a question of . . . how many moments can I fulfill? Can I dig down into deep places? If I can't, the moments don't work."

Those moments he spoke of turned on a deceptively simple structure. The play begins with Shannon in deep trouble for dallying with a young female member of his tour. He has sabotaged the bus as a means of forestalling his ultimate dismissal. The small group ends up in a shabby hotel in a Mexican coastal village. An old lover of Shannon's, Maxine, is the widowed owner of the hotel. They are joined by yet another beautiful woman, Hannah (a sketch artist), along with Hannah's father, an aging poet.

Chamberlain was attracted to the role of Shannon because the character had "big problems. There is a wonderful feeling of release in playing a part like that. . . . There are deep areas of pain and need and fear—and sometimes love."

Iguana rages with a boiling energy and Shannon is at the very center of it. He's a demanding character, difficult to play. But Joseph Hardy said, "Even when he [Chamberlain] might get exasperated either with himself or with another actor, he doesn't show it. He doesn't inflict it on other people."

Chamberlain's reputation for coolness under pressure is legendary. He rarely loses his temper. Jack Ryland, who played Bolingbroke in the Jonathan Miller productions of *Richard II,* said, "He doesn't deport himself like a star. He has gentility—a likable quality that comes across strong the minute you meet him."

Dorothy McGuire, who played Hannah to Chamberlain's

Shannon, perhaps best described the experience of working with him. "He has an extra quality," she began. "The thing that is remarkable about him is that he is truly an actor who does not have an ego problem. . . . No matter what he does or what might happen to him, he has a very positive outlook on life. . . . He's refreshing."

Miss McGuire, who had a long and illustrious film career, starring in such Hollywood films as *The Spiral Staircase, Till the End of Time,* and *A Summer Place,* was not the only name actor to join the cast of *Iguana* in Los Angeles. Eleanor Parker, another Hollywood leading lady with impressive credits in movies such as *Caged, The Seventh Sin,* and *Home from the Hill,* played Maxine. The most memorable member of the supporting cast, however, was an old and venerable actor whose name on the cast list assuredly brought nostalgic audiences to the theater in droves. That actor was Raymond Massey.

Chamberlain and his mentor were reunited this one last time on stage. For those who saw them act together a decade after *Dr. Kildare* went off the air, the feeling of warmth and respect between the two men added immeasurably to the experience.

The play was a huge success in Los Angeles, both critically and commercially. Plans were made to bring it to Broadway, and a year later the deed was done, but not without some considerable changes in the cast. Sadly, Raymond Massey had become too ill to make the trip to New York. Eleanor Parker didn't join the New York cast either, and she was replaced by two-time Oscar nominee Sylvia Miles (nominated for *Midnight Cowboy* and *Farewell My Lovely*). Joseph Hardy stayed on board as director for the new staging at the Circle in the Square theater, and Dorothy McGuire continued in her role as Hannah.

Except for the ill-fated *Breakfast at Tiffany's,* which never officially opened, *The Night of the Iguana* was Chamberlain's first time on Broadway.

"I always dreamed of doing a play on the New York stage," said Chamberlain. Though the dream came true, there were a few nightmarish moments during his run on the Great White Way. He called them "bizarre," and indeed they were. Inexplicably, chairs collapsed on stage when people sat down on them. One time when that happened, he said, "I looked down. There's Dorothy McGuire flat on the floor." They ended up laughing through their scene as he tried to pick her up. There was another time when, in one scene, he had his hands tied together. He was supposed to be able to untie himself but he couldn't get the knot undone.

There were, of course, the usual snafus. For instance, Sylvia Miles recalled, "There were two beach boys that worked for Maxine at the hotel. And one night one of them didn't show up, which kind of threw off Shannon's entrance. And I had to do his lines," she said, laughing at the memory.

According to Chamberlain, the most outrageous event during the New York run occurred when, one night, "a drunk lady starts yelling 'Bring on Dorothy McGuire!' before the show starts. They called the police who never came, having something better to do. Dorothy solved it by taking the lady on stage and saying, 'I want you to meet a fellow human being,' at which the audience cheered. It was so like Tennessee Williams!"

Chamberlain was particularly in tune with the playwright's style, but not altogether in agreement with his message in *Iguana*. Chamberlain and Williams met and discussed the play in some depth. "I think I have more hope for him [Shannon] than Tennessee does," said the actor. "I see him as a victim of his own system of unrealities. He thinks of himself as a kind of lover, but he's not. He's terrified of human relations.

"He thinks of himself as made superior by his potential godliness—well, his priestliness. It's a myth," he continued, explaining his interpretation of Shannon. "The degree of his self-deception is astronomical. The play is his voyage from a kind of tortured dislocation toward a beginning of actually seeing himself.

"Hannah opens him up by being absolutely naked in her honesty in the last scene and then sort of rejects him. He has always been so self-centered. But he is actually kind to her at that moment. I like to leave the possibility open that he and Maxine will pull it off somehow."

Williams, on the contrary, believed that Shannon was thoroughly destroyed by the end of the play and would not be saved by the love of Maxine. The actor and the playwright agreed to disagree, respecting each others' points of view. And by all accounts, Williams was quite pleased with the Chamberlain production of *Iguana*.

So were the critics. Chamberlain's Broadway debut was a smashing success with the press as well as with the public. Sylvia Miles recalled, "This particular production sold out and they wanted to extend it, but it couldn't be extended because Richard had a commitment afterward. It was to go to Australia . . . I think I'm kind of responsible, in a way, for that, because I had introduced him to a friend of mine who was putting together that project for *The Last Wave*."

For Chamberlain, the call of the movies was, as we explained, especially strong in the 1970s. Yet he put quite a lot of time in the middle 1970s into *The Night of the Iguana*. Even later, when television became the main focus of his career, Chamberlain continued to take time out to work on the stage.

In 1978, after his short but well-paid stint in *The Swarm*, the actor took on the role of Wild Bill Hickock in the Thomas Babe play *Fathers and Sons*. The play had a short run off-Broadway at New York's famed Public Theater, and was later revived with Chamberlain again in the lead role at the Solari Theater in Beverly Hills.

Thomas Babe's play concerns the last hours of Wild Bill's life before he is killed by a man who turns out to be his illegitimate son. The two men confront each other and their relationship is slowly revealed during the course of the drama.

"I had never played a part like this before," said Chamberlain, describing his interest in the Hickock role. "He's such a macho guy. I usually play more sensitive type people. All this swagger and gunplay and scaring people to death quality is something I haven't played before." Of course, Chamberlain had played plenty of characters with swagger (during his Dumas period), but he hadn't played anyone quite so crusty. There was nothing in the Hickock character to suggest the nobility and sophistication of all the period pieces the actor had starred in. Wild Bill was a rough-and-tumble character who talked the way you would expect an old Westerner to talk—and that was worlds apart from Lord Byron, Tchaikovsky, Louis XIV, etc. And no doubt it was good training for Chamberlain's later role in *Centennial*.

There were other advantages, as well, in working in *Fathers and Sons*. Virtually all of Chamberlain's theater work had been in revivals of famous works. From *Hamlet* to *The Lady's Not for Burning*, and from *Cyrano de Bergerac* to *The Night of the Iguana*, Chamberlain had worked in tried-and-true material. The Thomas Babe play was an original, and that meant the actor was willing to take greater chances.

Chamberlain continued taking chances of yet another kind

when he decided he wanted to direct, rather than star, in *The Shadow Box* at the Williamstown Theater Festival. The play had won both a Tony award and the Pulitzer prize for its author, Michael Cristofer. Curiously, Chamberlain has not been the only actor drawn to direct this compelling play about three dying people and their relationships to their families. The drama was turned into a movie in 1980 with Paul Newman directing. Perhaps both actor-directors were drawn to the material because the play's enormously theatrical structure makes it just as much a director's vehicle as it is an actor's showcase.

Whatever Chamberlain's reason for choosing *The Shadow Box,* the directing job had a powerful impact upon him. It helped refocus his interest in acting not so much as a career but as a craft. Soon after his experience up at Williamstown, he said, "There seem to be directions that have this great momentum in my life and I don't question them too closely. Like the whole directing thing has just opened up and I know that's going to be important for me. I have a feeling I'm going to end up teaching. I'm getting so excited about the process of acting. . . . Watching actors work and trying to help them draw a character . . . urging actors to stay with the reality of what they want . . . it's almost like having children."

Given Chamberlain's career-long dedication to his art, it isn't at all surprising that he might ultimately choose to teach young people the skills of the actor's craft. But the most immediate effect the directing experience seemed to have on Chamberlain was to pinpoint his *own* failings as an actor. Thanks to directing, he could more readily see exactly what he was doing wrong, himself, on the stage. Staying "with the reality" of a character is the hardest element in any performance and, at Williamstown, Chamberlain saw that with crystal clarity.

Though he never directed again, Chamberlain returned to

the Williamstown Theater Festival in the early 1980s to star in George Bernard Shaw's *Arms and the Man*. It was yet another stage triumph. But his most difficult and demanding theater performance was still before him. . . .

One blockbuster TV miniseries after another consumed Chamberlain's time and energies during the bulk of the 1980s. But just as he made time for *The Night of the Iguana* during his movie years, he made room for another Broadway play during his TV years.

"The theater is like home," he said. "I mean, you're right there with the audience instead of playing to a machine . . . but I haven't been on Broadway for ten years," he lamented.

In 1987, however, he came back to star in a revival of Noël Coward's *Blithe Spirit*. At the center of the play is a writer, Charles Condomine, who, in the course of researching a book on spiritualism, invites a medium (today they call them channels) to his home to conduct a séance. During the séance, Condomine's first wife is conjured up, but then she simply will not leave. Only Condomine can see and talk to her, causing both trouble with his second wife, and laughter (one hopes) in the audience. The play's basic plot line has become the stuff of TV sitcoms, but it was the playwright's urbane and witty dialogue that carried the piece and made it famous.

Coward wrote the play in six days in early 1941, and before the year was out, it had been a hit on both sides of the Atlantic, playing in New York for 657 performances with Clifton Webb in the role of Charles Condomine. The play won the New York Drama Critic's Circle award, but that was not the end of the show's success. It was made into a commercially and critically successful film in 1945 with Rex Harrison as the haunted author. Oddly, though, *Blithe Spirit* was never revived on Broadway during Coward's lifetime, and the

1987 production was the very first time it had played on Broadway since it originally opened in 1941.

Coward's heirs had refused to allow a Broadway production of the play unless a glittering cast could be arranged. When famed Oscar-winning actress Geraldine Page agreed to play Madame Arcati, the eccentric medium, the show's anchor had been established and the rest of the roles were quickly filled. In addition to Page, the cast boasted Blythe Danner (as the conjured, sexy first wife) and Judith Ivey (as the more staid second wife). Chamberlain (who played Charles Condomine) said his decision to join the cast was instantaneous. "They called up and said, 'How would you like to do *Blithe Spirit* with Geraldine Page?'" recalled the actor. "I said, 'Yes.' I didn't pause for a second. I think Geraldine is one of the very rare pure geniuses of acting of the theater. And working with her is just wonderful," he told an interviewer when the play opened.

Unfortunately, the production was troubled from the very start. "The out-of-town performances in Baltimore were a little shaky," admitted Chamberlain. "The style of Noel Coward is very hard to find now," he explained. "I don't know anybody who has a cigarette holder in one hand and a martini in the other and says fabulously witty things all the time. . . . You can't say lines like 'Would you like me to writhe at your feet in a frenzy of self-abasement?' and be a yuppie. . . . The one thing we don't want to do is prance around the stage like a bunch of nervous little whippets, trying to be terribly, terribly sophisticated and 'Oh, darling this and darling that' and all that stuff, because none of us can do it."

Chamberlain went on to say, "I think Noel Coward is the most difficult material in all of theater as far as I know. . . . It's like a juggling act—if you drop one ball, everything falls apart. Noel Coward is more difficult than Shakespeare . . . because the material is so gossamer thin. Shakespeare is robust, hearty, human material. Noel Coward is very, very light. . . . Shakespeare is like Roman stone work compared to these effervescent butterfly wings that Coward is made up of. You can read Shakespearean lines almost badly and they'll work. But you have to read Coward with such precision. . . . I've seen great, great actors fall flat on their faces in Noel Coward."

Chamberlain was anything but a great actor when he took his first turn at Coward. "I did *Private Lives* in summer stock right after *Dr. Kildare,*" he said, "and I don't think anybody has ever been worse in anything. I went in thinking it would be fun and frolic and very easy because it's so funny. Well, was I in for a surprise. I didn't do one thing right. I allowed myself to be completely dominated by the image of Noel Coward playing the part, and I tried to be Noel Coward, which is absolutely wrong."

It's interesting to note that Chamberlain actually met the playwright in London during the actor's British period. "I was afraid he might have caught an episode of *Dr. Kildare* and destroy me," said Chamberlain, "but he was very sweet."

Perhaps having met the man made approaching his work less intimidating. In any event, the actor was finally ready to tackle what he considered the theater's most difficult playwright, hoping to get a handle on Charles Condomine by approaching him as a realistic character rather than just a fountain of witty remarks.

Yet despite all the experience culled from more than twenty years of acting between his two tries at Coward's plays, the necessary light touch continued to elude him. The show played out of town in Baltimore and Washington, but the production simply wouldn't jell. "It was a real slog through rehearsals," said Chamberlain. "Very, very difficult work."

Chamberlain wasn't the only one having difficulties. Eventually, the production's director, Brian Bedford, quit before the play opened in New York. Brian Murray, who had directed a successful revival of Coward's *Hay Fever* the previous year, took over the helm of *Blithe Spirit,* delaying the opening two weeks while he and the cast worked diligently to try to bring the play up to its bubbly potential.

Murray told his cast, "When you play Coward and you're on top of the material it's an absolute joy, like surfing on an endless set of waves or driving a Porsche. It's a thrilling, exhilarating experience."

During rehearsals, the play's producers came up with a clever publicity stunt, inviting a practicing medium, Mr. David Vass, to the theater to have a séance (à la Madame Arcati) in order to predict the show's future. Mr. Vass reportedly went into a trance and said that the stars would win Tony awards and that the play would be a hit. His predictions were woefully incorrect.

After opening night, Frank Rich of *The New York Times* wrote, "Four first-rate actors—all except Blythe Danner miscast, none in top form—struggle for three acts to find the light touch that might make this lark . . . take flight. The efforts grow more desperate as the night stretches to trance-inducing length. . . . When a Coward witticism occasionally does emerge unscathed in this *Blithe Spirit,* chances are that it is spoken by the relatively restrained Mr. Chamberlain or Miss Danner. Sporting a tux and, to stiffen his upper lip, a mustache, Mr. Chamberlain brings much effort and skill to the effort of capturing the Coward persona embodied by Charles. But the role is not a natural fit—which it must be with this playwright—and the actor snaps too many of his flippant lines too hard, hurling rather than floating them. Only at the end, when a liberated Charles declares that he's at last enjoying himself 'immensely,' does Mr. Chamberlain fully relax and seem to find some pleasure in his assignment."

Clive Barnes of the *New York Post* was no less kind to the

play, but considerably harder on Chamberlain. "Almost everything . . . is subtly but crucially wrong," he said. Director Brian Murray, wrote Barnes, "has difficulty persuading the actors to speak their lines clearly, and without phony nuance. The worst offender is the usually worthy Richard Chamberlain as a disastrous Charles."

The *Daily News* lined up with the other three New York newspapers on the play. Chamberlain, critic Howard Kissel wrote, "looks debonair as the writer, but his jauntiness is effortful. Flippancy should not require so much work."

Following his long-standing, self-protective practice, Chamberlain refused to read the reviews. "I get people to tell me pertinent things from them," he said. "If I read them, it's too frightening . . ."

The reviews weren't all bad. For instance, the local CBS critic called the play "A knockout! A sheer delight." But the critical comments—whether good or bad—finally didn't matter to the public. And in that sense, the medium, Mr. Vass, had been right about the show being a hit. Theatergoers continued buying tickets, and the originally announced limited run for the show was extended.

It was easy to see why bad reviews didn't hurt the production's box office. The all-star cast had legitimate drawing power. The best evidence of that were the sounds of squealing women in the audience when Chamberlain made his entrance. Even in his early fifties, seen in person, the bond between the star and his female audience remained unbroken.

It was during the extended-run period of the play that tragedy struck the *Blithe Spirit* company. Without any warning, Geraldine Page died of a heart attack. It was a shock to the entertainment industry, which lost one of its most admired and cherished performers. She had won her first Oscar (after seven nominations) just the year before for *The Trip to Bountiful,* and film and theater people gathered from all over

America for a memorial service in her honor. Chamberlain praised her in the eulogy he offered at the service which was, most appropriately, held in the theater.

With the loss of Geraldine Page, the play quickly closed. *Blithe Spirit* had become a memory that was anything but blithe. It is the last play that Chamberlain has performed in, to date.

19

THE MAN WHO WOULD BE KING

The hallmark of Chamberlain's career has been his willingness—even eagerness—to work in several media, and to work at all levels of those media. For instance, in his stage work, he has performed in regional theaters, off-Broadway, and Broadway. In the movies, he has done big Hollywood commercial films, all-star movies, art films, musicals, farces, and adventure yarns. But he has shown his greatest versatility and has had his greatest successes in the medium of his beginnings: television.

Chamberlain has been a towering star in every aspect of prime-time TV. He was a megastar of a top-rated series, he has lent his name and talent to first-class PBS productions, he has been the lead in several impressive made-for-TV movies, and his crowning glory has been his reign as the monarch of the miniseries.

Ask the average person what they know about Richard Chamberlain, and if they're old enough, they'll likely mention *Dr. Kildare, Shogun,* and *The Thorn Birds.* Ask a younger person about Chamberlain, and you'll only hear about the mini-series. His impact as a star has clearly been on TV. His theater triumphs have enhanced his image within the industry, but it is his work on the tube that has enhanced his image with the public.

While not all of his TV projects have been winners either artistically or commercially, they have all been enormously ambitious. In fact, when he talks about the medium that nurtured his talents and gave him his start, Chamberlain becomes a bit evangelical. It's as if he views his work on the tube as a mission. "I'm an actor," he said, "who feels a great obligation to TV. It's been very good to me. I don't think it should be sneered at by my profession. God forbid those millions who watch it should never get the chance to see anything good . . . I know most of it is awful but it won't get any better unless we do something about it."

Most working actors don't watch very much television; they're usually working day and night and have no time for it. But Chamberlain had an experience in the early 1980s that typified his feelings toward TV. "Someone gave me two kittens for my last birthday," he told an interviewer, "and when I was sitting in front of the TV one night they clambered up on my lap and fell asleep. I'd just got them and I didn't want to disturb them, so I had to sit through a new quiz show which had just come on. Well, I was mesmerized by the horror of it. I'd never seen anything as abysmally stupid. People must be given a chance to see something better."

It wasn't an empty, snobby statement. Chamberlain has marched his career into the breach, fighting to make the best television possible. His battleground has been the miniseries, which has been the front line of television's ratings wars.

"TV miniseries are a great forum for actors," Chamberlain declared. "The time and money lavished on miniseries make them very special. And the pace is good for actors—not as slow as films, not as fast as TV movies. . . . I love doing miniseries. It's a wonderful medium. As an actor, it gives me a lot of range."

When asked what his favorite miniseries is, however, one is surprised to learn that it isn't one of his own productions. His favorite is *Brideshead Revisited*. "I don't think it could be topped, or even equaled, by anyone," he proclaimed. "It was so brilliantly done, every little detail." Having worked in *Portrait of a Lady* for the BBC, Chamberlain was in a good position to compare American miniseries to the British, and he thinks the British do a better job of it. They "have been doing them for a long time," he said, "and I doubt we'll ever surpass them."

In some areas, the British *do* excel. When they make a miniseries out of a great piece of literature, or when they make a long-format mystery, nobody does it better. But when it comes to sweeping adventures and grand passions that appeal to huge audiences, the American miniseries is the champ. And Richard Chamberlain has been the star of more first-rate American minis than any other actor.

His miniseries career started in earnest in 1979 with the epic *Centennial,* based on the best-selling novel by James A. Michener. The story chronicled the eventual birth and growth of a small Colorado town called Centennial. Among the enormous number of well-known actors joining Chamberlain in the cast were William Atherton, Raymond Burr, Barbara Carrera, Robert Conrad, Richard Crenna, Timothy Dalton, Chief Dan George, Andy Griffith, Mark Harmon, Gregory Harrison, David Janssen (as the narrator), Brian Keith, Sally Kellerman, Stephen McHattie, Donald Pleasence, Lynn Redgrave, Pernell Roberts, Robert Vaughn, Clint Walker, Dennis Weaver, and Anthony Zerbe. It was an impressive gathering of actors, yet this TV spectacular was conceived for the small screen by writer and executive producer John Wilder not as an all-star film but as an intelligent, quality production. So, despite the celebrity turns, the drama generally came first and foremost.

Though *Centennial* was loaded with famous TV actors as well as up-and-coming stars, Chamberlain's character was at the heart and soul of the show. Though he appeared in only about half of the miniseries, his air time was, by far, the longest stretch of any actor in the production. And it was his presence that lent the entire show an undeniable air of dignity.

Centennial began during the mountain-man era of the early 1800s, introducing Chamberlain as a young Scotsman named Alexander McKeog. As an inexperienced trapper, Chamberlain's McKeog was a literal babe in the woods who would have had little chance for survival if not for his friendship with the French Canadian frontiersman, Pasquinel, played (in the best performance of his life) by Robert Conrad. The two characters, despite their deep differences, became close friends. But the Indian woman whom McKeog loved was married to Pasquinel, and there, in that simple triangle, was the engine that set everything else in the miniseries into motion.

Conrad's flamboyant, earthy performance was the perfect foil for Chamberlain's reserved, tentative McKeog. The two actors had a lively chemistry on screen that made the first part of the miniseries come wonderfully to life. After Pasquinel died and that chemistry was lost, Chamberlain's strength as an actor was put to the test. He had to bring something new to his role in order to fill the emotional gap left by Pasquinel's demise. He rose to the challenge, totally dominating the show every night, hour after hour, with an intense, regal majesty that came from his link to Pasquinel and the grand, wild, free past of his youth that no man would ever experience again. In other words, he internalized the chemistry he had had with Conrad and continued to make it work for him as an actor.

Centennial received mixed reviews from TV critics when it was aired, but it was quite popular with audiences, although nothing compared to Chamberlain's next two miniseries, *Shogun* and *The Thorn Birds*. Despite the huge popularity of those later minis and the fascinating and complex characters he portrayed in them, of those three men it was Alexander McKeog that Chamberlain particularly enjoyed playing. "He was one of the kind of people I admire most," said the actor. And why not? McKeog was loyal to his friends, loving to his wife, caring about the land, and above all else, at peace with himself.

In retrospect, *Centennial* marked the enthronement of Chamberlain as "king of the miniseries." Say what you will about the title—Chamberlain hates it—his reign over the better part of a decade, in terms of quality television, has been nothing less than royal.

20

SAMURAI ACTOR

There has hardly been a more ambitious miniseries on a commercial American TV network than *Shogun*. The very idea of presenting twelve hours of prime-time television with long stretches of dialogue in Japanese (without any subtitles) took enormous corporate courage. But James Clavell's novel had been a monster hit in bookstores, and NBC was willing to gamble that viewers would tune in to see how this sweeping historical saga would be translated into a visual story.

Jerry London, the director of *Shogun*, said, "What we have here is *Earthquake*, *The Towering Inferno*, *Gone with the Wind*, and *Intolerance*—all in one." There was a surprising amount of truth in that broad statement. There were natural disasters in the *Shogun* script, including a massive earthquake; the movie was certainly meant to be a crowd pleaser in the tradition of *The Towering Inferno*; it had a great love story like *Gone with the Wind*; and it had both the huge budget (at a staggering $22 million) and some of the artistic intentions of D. W. Griffith's silent masterpiece, *Intolerance*.

That such a project would end up on TV didn't faze Eric Bercovici, the screenwriter and producer of the miniseries, who said, "Television, surprisingly enough, is far more daring than movies. TV will take a chance."

In 1980, the year *Shogun* was broadcast, NBC was in the ratings cellar and was more willing than most to take the gamble on a controversial miniseries. Unlike a production such as *Centennial,* however, *Shogun* didn't have the advantage of a huge cast list of familiar TV actors. Chamberlain was the only bona fide American star in the show. There were plenty of Japanese stars, however, such as the legendary Toshiro Mifune and the hugely popular (in Japan) Yoko Shimada. But their presence in the production wasn't expected to have any effect on the Nielsen ratings.

It was up to Chamberlain to help bring in the viewers. Yet he was not the first choice to play Pilot Major John Blackthorne. He had read the novel roughly three years before the miniseries was aired, and he had pursued the role, feeling certain that it would be a terrific TV project. James Clavell, who not only wrote the novel, but was acting as the miniseries' executive producer, wanted either Sean Connery or Albert Finney to play the lead. While Finney was never seriously considered by NBC, Sean Connery was. And Connery was interested in the part. At the last minute, however, due to scheduling conflicts, he had to withdraw from the project.

Chamberlain was finally given full consideration for the role of Blackthorne. Clavell was initially horrified at the prospect of the former Dr. Kildare playing the hero of his story. In the end, though, Clavell, as well as a massive TV audience, was thrilled by Chamberlain's performance as Pilot Blackthorne and can now hardly imagine anyone else in the role.

Chamberlain was officially offered the part just one scant week before the six-and-a-half-month shooting schedule began in Japan. For his part, Chamberlain said, "I was terrified of doing *Shogun*. But that sense of danger was what made me want to do it."

In its simplest form, the story of *Shogun* told the tale of an Englishman who piloted a Dutch sailing vessel that was shipwrecked on the Japanese coast. The year was 1600. The viewer learned the ways of feudal Japan along with Blackthorne, as he became involved in the power politics of the Japanese lords. And the viewer also felt the poignancy of Blackthorne's love for a beautiful Japanese woman, a love that was doomed to failure.

Chamberlain's method of getting inside his character and learning the part was the same as always. "I read the script hundreds of times," he said, "looking for clues—hints about what's going on inside. What the character wants . . . what he's trying to make people do, what he needs. If, God forbid, it's a historical character, I read as much information about him as possible."

Blackthorne's saga was based on the real-life William Adams, the first Englishman in Japan, so Chamberlain studied not only the script and Clavell's novel, he also read about Adams and early seventeenth-century Japan. Unfortunately, after he won the role, there was little time left to delve any deeper. His schedule simply wouldn't allow for it. According to Eric Bercovici, "He worked 125 days of the 130-day shooting schedule . . . and he was never unprepared."

Chamberlain appeared in nearly all of the more than one thousand scenes in the entire twelve-hour production. In addition, he also filmed separate scenes that were used to help bridge gaps in the story in order to make a two-hour film version of the miniseries that was shown theatrically in the rest of the world.

In America, *Shogun* was critically acclaimed, and more than fulfilled NBC's ratings hopes, becoming one of the most watched miniseries of all time. It was truly a television masterpiece, marred only by an abrupt ending that was less than satisfactory. Chamberlain's popularity soared as a result of the miniseries and, suddenly, just as in the *Kildare* days, he found himself besieged by autograph-seekers. And no wonder. His performance, in a complex and difficult role, was genuinely magnificent. Among the obstacles he had to overcome were a mostly Japanese cast, which meant he often had to play against actors with whom he couldn't verbally communicate, and a story construction that demanded that the vast majority of his scenes be reactive, rather than active. Because of the length and breadth of the miniseries, he had to play a staggering range of emotions. Surprisingly, he didn't win an Emmy for his performance, though he was, indeed, nominated.

"What you get from Richard Chamberlain that you don't get from most television actors," said Eric Bercovici, "is a true performance. He is a real pro." As proof of this, the producer explained that during the entire course of the shooting schedule in Japan, he and Chamberlain had only one serious disagreement. "Richard felt he had not done his best work in one scene," said Bercovici, "and so he wrote me a letter, clearly and carefully outlining what we should do. He was right. We changed everything, but not because Richard used any kind of emotional threat. He does not throw tantrums."

There were other things that Chamberlain would have liked to have changed in *Shogun*, but they were not within his ability to affect. For instance, though he had great respect for Toshiro Mifune, he felt that the Japanese actor was rigid in his interpretation of Lord Toranaga. "Mifune-san is a wonderful actor," said Chamberlain, "but I'm not sure that anything I do, on or off camera, will change his performance at all."

On a more personal note, Chamberlain lamented his inability to communicate with so many of his coworkers in *Shogun*. Though he was in Japan for more than six months, "I was too stupid and busy to learn the language," he said. "At the wrap party," he continued, "five Japanese people told me, in English, how much they liked me. They never spoke to me because they didn't want to speak English poorly. I regretted that. We could have been great buddies."

Centennial had been an important step in Chamberlain's miniseries career, but *Shogun* instantly put him at the top of the heap. He was well aware of his new clout, and that's why he then created his own production company which he called Cham Enterprises. "Cham" was not only a shortened version of Chamberlain, it was also the name he had always used to sign his paintings and other artworks ever since he was a student at Pomona College.

His own production plans aside, Chamberlain was much in demand by others. Following his spectacular success in *Shogun*, Chamberlain was tapped to cohost the 1980–81 Tony awards show with Ellen Burstyn. As both a popular TV actor and as a genuinely committed stage actor, he was the perfect choice and he did an admirable job.

In 1981, as Chamberlain looked to his future, he said, "What I want to do is get back to playing leading men again. *Shogun* gave me the chance to do that—a marvelous part—and I want to continue." The role he might have had in mind was that of Father Ralph de Bricassart in Colleen Mc-Cullough's international best-seller, *The Thorn Birds*.

21

A PRIEST, A GIRL, AND A MEGA-HIT

*T*he *Thorn Birds* is a saga of forbidden love about an ambitious priest and the beautiful young girl who wins his heart. Spanning the years from 1915 to the late 1960s, and set against the backdrop of a rugged, developing Australia, *The Thorn Birds* was that rare gem of a story that was graced with real people and real emotions. The characters—all of them—were flawed human beings who were all the more touching because they weren't entirely heroic or evil.

The story revolved around Father Ralph de Bricassart, a handsome priest who refused the sexual advances of an aging, powerful Australian woman (Barbara Stanwyck). At her death she had a perverse revenge, however, when she left her ranch, Drogheda, to the church, unalterably tying Father Ralph to Stanwyck's young niece, little Meggie, a girl to whom the priest had become especially attached.

When Meggie became a young woman, Father Ralph couldn't help falling in love with her, despite his vow of celibacy. Eventually, he broke his vow in order to test his love of the church. After a romantic idyll, Ralph finally chose God over Meggie without ever knowing that he had left her pregnant. It wasn't until the end of his life, when the young man who was Ralph's son died, that the priest learned the shattering truth.

It was no wonder that Colleen McCollough's novel was a hit; *The Thorn Birds* was a heartstopping love story. And Chamberlain immediately saw its miniseries potential. "I knew when it first came out *Thorn Birds* would be a great television show," Chamberlain reflected, "and I was disappointed when I heard it was being planned as a theatrical film." He didn't believe it would make nearly as good a movie as it would a miniseries. As much as he wanted the lead role of Father Ralph, he knew that his limited drawing power as a major movie star would not be enough to land him the part.

Ironically, Robert Redford, who had vied with Chamberlain for the role of Dr. Kildare more than twenty years earlier, was the prime candidate to play the priest torn between his devotion to the church and his desire for Meggie. With all due respect to Redford, Chamberlain would have been a better casting decision even for the movie version. While both possessed the charm and sexual appeal to play Meggie's lover, only Chamberlain exuded the spirituality that was the other half of Father Ralph's personality.

Despite Redford's interest in the project, Chamberlain still might have held out some hope of being cast in the movie version, because Peter Weir, who directed him in *The Last Wave,* was slated to direct *The Thorn Birds.* Eventually, though, Weir dropped out of the project, as did two other distinguished film directors, Arthur Hiller and Herbert Ross. They all tried and failed to come up with a script that worked at the shorter length required for movie theaters. In the end, even a four-hour extravaganza couldn't do the story justice.

David Wolper, the executive producer of *The Thorn Birds* miniseries, later said, "There is a certain kind of book that shouldn't be a theatrical film. Michener's *Hawaii* was one of those. *Thorn Birds* is another—too long, too rich."

Once the decision was made to make *The Thorn Birds* into an ABC miniseries, a whole new slew of actors were considered for the role of Father Ralph. After his success in *Shogun*, Chamberlain became a leading contender, but he hardly had the part locked up. He reportedly had strong competition from, among others, Christopher Reeve and Peter Strauss. Among television miniseries stars, Strauss had just as much clout as Chamberlain in getting the premiere roles.

"As an actor," said Chamberlain to an interviewer, explaining the appeal of Father Ralph, "the biggest reason I like the role is that it is a great challenge to portray a man in this extraordinary dilemma; a man whose heart is torn in half in a lifelong struggle." But his attraction to the role was finally more personal than that. After reading the book, "something turned in my gut. Only later did I realize the amazing parallels. Ralph's big problem is his image. Like me, trying to live up to an image. Ralph falls into that trap of wanting to be the perfect priest and wanting to have the perfect relationship with God, and I really relate to that. It's a crucial problem for Ralph and it's a crucial problem for me. Ralph strives for his image of perfection and he keeps failing and it drives him crazy. Finally, he gets chopped down and he realizes he is a flawed human being. And then he is free."

In a reprise of the casting scenario for *Shogun*, the role of Father Ralph in *The Thorn Birds* wasn't cast until just two weeks before shooting was scheduled to begin. When Chamberlain received word that he had won the part, he immediately threw a party for all of his friends in Los Angeles.

He joined a cast that included Barbara Stanwyck, Jean Simmons, Richard Kiley, Mare Winningham, Christopher

Plummer, Philip Anglim, Ken Howard, Bryan Brown, and Rachel Ward as Meggie. Unlike *Shogun*, however, *The Thorn Birds* was not shot on location. Instead of filming in Australia, the ten-hour, $21 million miniseries was filmed in California.

For once, Chamberlain wasn't gallivanting all over the world. He was on a different sort of journey; an inner journey. Chamberlain sensed a certain fate in his getting the role of Father Ralph. "When you need to work out something in your life," he said, "you seem to attract the part that will help you do it."

He wanted to get in touch with his emotions, become less aloof. Later, he said, "I think I needed that role for my own life at the time. I'm hoping to get more vulnerable, learn to express need."

What he needed in particular during the filming of *The Thorn Birds* was a great deal of patience. He had only one week of rehearsals before beginning five and a half months of shooting on a production that was soon beset by a great many problems.

For instance, Barbara Stanwyck was unhappy at the prospect of having some of her lines cut and she fought over it with the producer, Stan Margulies. But Rachel Ward reportedly caused the greatest number of problems on the set. The former model was, according to Chamberlain, "scared to death the first couple of weeks." Ward admitted, "I was miserable a lot of the time." And she made much of the cast miserable, as well, with (in Liz Smith's words) "her high-handed attitude." Once she began her love affair with Bryan Brown, her Australian costar (and eventually her husband), "she seemed to get happier and happier, and her work got better and better," said Chamberlain.

Barbara Stanwyck and Rachel Ward weren't the only ones having problems on the set. Chamberlain himself was terribly unhappy about the lack of development in his character. In a rare outburst of frustration, he broke his hand by slamming his fist into a chair. "I haven't done anything this stupid in ten years," he told Mary Murphy, writing for *TV Guide*. "What happened on the set is that I carried my anger too far. I would say that breaking my hand was going too far," he added archly. "It certainly wasn't healthy. I hurt myself. What I really wanted to do was to yell at somebody else," he explained. "There is an area of the script that I have been complaining about for a long time. I'm not getting anywhere. I don't feel I am being listened to. So, I broke my hand."

Chamberlain had been unhappy with the way his relationship with Meggie was written. He believed that Father Ralph's sexual attraction for Meggie was a monumental soul-searching event, whereas, said the actor, "the writer [Carmen Culver] and director [Daryl Duke] saw it as something very casual."

Finally, the three of them met and, Chamberlain reported, "We argued for four hours. It was what I had always wanted to do—release a lot of energy in terms of anger and frustration at the people who were responsible for this area of the script. After the argument I felt great. I made my points. They made theirs. We compromised, and the lull in my acting just disappeared."

The outburst and its aftermath also seemed to be the answer to Chamberlain's desire to show more emotion, to be less aloof. He was letting his anger out and it was not only cathartic for the actor, it helped make *The Thorn Birds* a better miniseries. But it was not, in Chamberlain's opinion, his best. Though he found Father Ralph to be one of his most challenging, difficult roles, "in the sense of being the most complicated and paradoxical person I've had to play," he ultimately wasn't satisfied with his character. "[Ralph] wasn't fully developed in either the book or screenplay, which presented difficulties," said the actor. "You never really saw

Ralph at work . . . and I missed that. It would have given me a chance to show more clearly why Ralph was more committed to the church than to Meggie."

His own criticism notwithstanding, *The Thorn Birds* was a considerable storytelling achievement. It didn't falter at the end, the way *Shogun* did, nor did it meander through too many characters and subplots as did *Centennial*. When it aired in early 1983, the critics adored it and a vast TV audience that numbered roughly 110 million wished it would never end.

Chamberlain earned his third Emmy nomination in eight years for his work as Father Ralph. But he lost yet again. He took the setback well, however, saying, "Awards—good grief, they're not even the icing, they're a candle on the cake. You can't be in this business for awards." But Chamberlain is a competitive type, and he finally admitted his disappointment. "It was like preparing for opening night and they decided to cancel the performance," he said.

22

MAKING HISTORY

*A*fter the personal triumphs of *Centennial, Shogun,* and *The Thorn Birds,* Chamberlain once again did the unexpected when he chose to co-star with Rod Steiger in a made-for-TV movie, *Cook and Peary: The Race to the Pole.* Signing on to act in a film that would be broadcast merely one single evening must have seemed like a vacation for Chamberlain after the extraordinary long shooting schedules for his three previous miniseries. Appearances, however, were undoubtedly deceiving. Making *Cook and Peary* was anything but a vacation.

As he had so many times in the past, Chamberlain chose to recreate the life of a historical figure, playing Frederick A. Cook, a physician who traded in his white coat and stethoscope for the snowshoes and dogsled of an Arctic explorer. The TV movie was built around the relationship between Dr. Cook and his one-time friend, Admiral Robert E. Peary (Rod Steiger). After the two men had a falling out, they became fierce competitors, each of them trying to become the first man to reach the North Pole. Both men claimed they reached their destination before the other, but Peary is generally credited with having won the race.

The movie was shot in Canada and the frozen reaches of the North Atlantic. When Chamberlain looked out upon the windswept ice off the coast of Greenland, he understood why the two explorers were drawn to the Arctic wasteland. "It must have been like walking into God's house," he said.

And God nearly invited him home for the rest of eternity. . . .

During the shoot, Chamberlain and fifteen other cast and crew members had turned an ice floe into a movie set. Suddenly, there was a great roaring sound. The giant block of ice broke away from its position and began to float out to sea. No longer stable, the ice floe began to disintegrate underneath their feet.

Word of this disaster in the making brought immediate help in the form of a helicopter that soon swooped down to save the stranded actors and crew. Producer Robert Halmi said, "They were plucked to safety just in the nick of time. Moments after they were removed from the ice, the platform broke apart."

The only other major danger that Chamberlain faced while making *Cook and Peary* was whenever he was in a scene with Rod Steiger. The volcanic Steiger, a famous method actor, had considerably different working habits than did Chamberlain. Steiger's brooding, scene-chewing improvisations were a challenge to his classically trained costar; it was a battle of acting styles that Chamberlain clearly enjoyed. "He's a legendary actor," said Chamberlain, speaking of Steiger, "and to find yourself in intense scenes with someone who is awe-inspiring, it puts one on one's toes.

"Rod improvised a lot, but he usually ends up with the right cue," continued Chamberlain. "I never worked before with anyone who does that, and it's nervous-making, but in a good way. You really have to listen. He kept saying things differently, and I thought, 'Well, that's interesting.' It's like there's a time bomb in him that could go off at any time. That's a wonderful quality for an actor."

Cook and Peary was shown on CBS on December 13, 1983. It was generally well received by the critics, but the slow-moving story was not a huge ratings success despite its stark beauty and the restrained performances by the two stars.

Even before *Cook and Peary* was made, Chamberlain was in hot pursuit of what would become his greatest miniseries role, another bigger-than-life human being from the pages of recent history: Raoul Wallenberg.

"Wallenberg was a fascinating guy," said Chamberlain, describing the historical basis of his next miniseries. "As a Swedish diplomat assigned to the embassy in Budapest, he became acquainted with the Jewish tragedy. Because of his position, Wallenberg could save Jews in the daytime and dine with [Nazi henchman] Adolf Eichmann at night. He was incredibly resourceful in dreaming up scams to free Jews. He could have been shot and yet continued his activities until he was arrested by the Russians on January 17, 1945. He disappeared into the Soviet Gulag, and was never seen again. The Russians claim he died in 1947 and yet someone reported spotting him in 1978. The family is still hopeful he's alive," he added earnestly.

With equal measures of heroism and panache, the Wallenberg tale is one of the most inspiring true stories of our time. Wallenberg saved—virtually single-handedly—100,000 Hungarian Jews by issuing fake "protective passes" that got them out of Nazi-occupied territory before they could be killed.

Plans had been under way for quite some time to make a miniseries of Wallenberg's wartime exploits, but the project was slow in developing. "I heard about it three and a half years ago," said Chamberlain around the time the two-part, four-hour miniseries finally aired in early 1985, "and knew I wanted to play Wallenberg. At the time it looked like another actor was going to get it. Then the project seemed to disappear, but NBC picked it up and that's when I became involved."

The full title of the miniseries was *Wallenberg: A Hero's Story*. In addition to Chamberlain as the lead character, the renowned Swedish actress, Bibi Andersson, played Wallenberg's mother, and Alice Krige, in the first of two costarring roles in Chamberlain miniseries, played Wallenberg's love interest, the Baroness Elizabeth Kemeny. Most interestingly, *Wallenberg* was written by Gerald Green, the same man who wrote the award-winning miniseries *Holocaust*.

The one flaw in *Wallenberg* was the artificial romance between the title character and the baroness. Curiously, though, while the love story tended to trivialize the larger drama, there were definite sparks between Chamberlain and Krige.

"I fell somewhat in love with Alice Krige when I saw her in *Chariots of Fire*," confided Chamberlain. "I hadn't seen an actress who glowed on film like that for a long time. Working with her was a dream. I would be happy working with her if I had to play all the rest of my love scenes with her, for the rest of my life. . . . I can't account for why we look so good together onscreen," he added. "The chemistry is an absolute mystery."

Krige felt the same delight in working with Chamberlain. "During the making of *Wallenberg*," she said, "I became enormously enamored of Richard. Not only is he a splendid actor, but he's a delightful man. . . . There is a foundation of trust and confidence between us that makes it a joy working with him."

Feeling as they did about each other, it was no wonder that they soon worked together again in *Dream West*.

Chamberlain's three earlier miniseries had been sweeping adventures and love stories. *Wallenberg* had those qualities, but it was also a production that deeply touched the spirit. Of all his miniseries, *Wallenberg* is Chamberlain's favorite. It is also his most accomplished work as a TV actor. The critics applauded the show and viewers tuned in to NBC in large numbers for two nights of the most dramatic and moving miniseries of the 1980s.

What followed, however, was one of the biggest outrages in Emmy history: Chamberlain wasn't even nominated for a Best Actor award. Fritz Weaver, who had worked with Chamberlain on *Dr. Kildare* and who costarred with him in his next miniseries, *Dream West,* said, "One of the finest performances of recent years was his performance in *Wallenberg.* I was just knocked out by what Richard did and I told him, 'Jesus, that was my favorite performance of last year.' He was very pleased because, for some reason, it was kind of overlooked when the Emmys were being handed out. I couldn't believe it," Weaver flared. "This man had paid his dues and worked through the years but this was a real performance; it was the real thing. And he played it in a different way than Richard normally does—Richard, of course, is this commodity as well as an actor. But he got out of that category of the juvenile and played a man of steely resolve and will—it was just wonderful."

Considering the fact that *Wallenberg* aired after the highly acclaimed miniseries *Holocaust* (in which Fritz Weaver happened to star), it becomes clearer why the Chamberlain two-parter was generally ignored by the Emmy voters. Perhaps the TV academy felt that they had already done their duty by giving awards to Gerald Green's previous production on a similar theme. In addition, *Holocaust* had been a particularly long miniseries, while *Wallenberg* was "merely" four hours. To some, *Wallenberg*'s shorter length might have been an excuse to give it equally short shrift. But whatever the reason for the oversight, Chamberlain's best work was not acknowledged by his peers.

Remarkably—and ironically—this man who is considered America's finest classical actor, who has won high praise for his work on stage, screen, and television, has yet to win a Tony, Oscar, or Emmy.

23

THE MONARCH MISSES

$\mathcal{F}$ rom *Centennial* through *Wallenberg,* Chamberlain's miniseries had been like a ratings juggernaut, smashing their way to top-ten lists with stunning regularity. It was no wonder that by the mid-1980s he was commonly known as "King of the Miniseries." Chamberlain's presence in a miniseries seemed like money in the bank to everyone concerned. Any producer who could sign him on as a star of a new project could write his own ticket with the networks.

Chuck McLain, the executive producer of *Dream West,* was well aware of Chamberlain's name value. He had the added advantage of being an old friend of the actor's, so when he read *Dream West,* a best-selling novel by David Nevin, he knew whom he wanted as his star.

Dream West had all the elements anyone could ask for in a gripping miniseries. There was action, romance, historical sweep, and above all else, a compelling true story about one of America's greatest, yet least known, heroes, John Charles Frémont.

The fact that Frémont was an unfamiliar name to the general public didn't deter McLain. When a reporter asked the executive producer if he was concerned about making a big-budget miniseries about "an unknown," McLain smartly replied, "Not when you cast Richard Chamberlain in the lead."

Frémont, however, wasn't just unknown to the mass audience. Chamberlain didn't know much about the nineteenth-century adventurer, either. But he learned fast.

"America was a little Eastern country when he started his push West," explained Chamberlain, warming to the subject of his newly researched character. "It was an imperialistic movement with Frémont in the forefront. He made the first really scientific maps and showed people how to get from Connecticut to Oregon safely. . . . It was Frémont who was directly responsible for bringing California into the Union. He and sixty men conquered California at the beginning of the Mexican-American War and he served as first governor of the state. . . . You could say he was in the fast lane of history."

The more he studied Frémont, the more he liked the role. "The key to Frémont, the thing that turns me on about him," said the actor, "is feeling his vitality. When I'm acting him, I feel in him this kind of racehorse vitality, enough vitality to change the world. Frémont changed his country. It's a wonderful thing to feel."

The man Chamberlain was playing had earned the nickname of "the Pathfinder." Frémont led five harrowing expeditions into the unknown Western territories, fought in two wars, was the first candidate for president of the new Republican party, made and lost several fortunes, and had a genuine lifelong love affair with his wife, Jessie, who tried to maximize the effects of her husband's impetuous derring-do.

According to Chamberlain, Jessie "ghost-wrote the journals of his expeditions. He described to her all his adventures and she wrote them out in this wonderful style that caught the imagination of the whole nation." Putting it in terms with which he was eminently familiar, Chamberlain explained the effect Frémont and his wife had on America by saying, "It was something akin to what Dr. Kildare did for medicine. Enrollment in medical schools was declining. Then *Dr. Kildare* and *Ben Casey* went on the air and enrollment zoomed up. When Frémont's journals were published, people packed their bags and got in their covered wagons and traveled west. Those journals probably speeded up the acquisition of the West by decades," he concluded.

By the time he was actually filming the miniseries, Chamberlain had become enormously enthused about playing John Charles Frémont, whom he would portray from the age of twenty-six to a ripe old seventy-four (covering the years 1839 to 1887). "I like this man a lot," Chamberlain declared. "I really like him! I like his naïveté. I like the qualities that got him in trouble. I like the fact that he wasn't a good politician, that he wasn't a good businessman. He didn't end up with any money, but he certainly ended up accomplishing a lot."

Nonetheless, there was a difference between playing historical figures like Raoul Wallenberg, F. Scott Fitzgerald, and King Edward, who greatly affected the lives of others but who didn't greatly change the course of history, and Frémont, who grandly altered a nation's destiny. There is a heavier responsibility for accuracy in playing such a role, and Chamberlain was well aware of it. But neither was he terribly bothered by it.

"I have mixed feelings about this kind of fictional history," said Chamberlain to Geoffrey C. Ward. "None of us has the same personality as another human being, and if I'm portraying another human being there's already distortion," he admitted. "Nobody knows what he was really like. On the other hand, there's enough truth in this, enough fact, to make it a better idea of Frémont than no idea at all. This film isn't interested in improving the consciousness of America," he candidly continued. "The people who are making this film are presenting a good, solid drama that will keep people watching the commercials. That's why this is being done. This isn't Frémont. It's facts about Frémont. I can't be exactly like him. That would just be futile, and I know the audience knows that."

The audience also knew that it was getting a big-budget frontier spectacle. The cost of making the seven-hour, three-part *Dream West* was $18 million, and every penny was evident in the lavish production.

Joining Chamberlain in the cast was Alice Krige as Jessie Benton, Fritz Weaver as Senator Thomas Hart Benton (Jessie's father), Rip Torn as Kit Carson, Anthony Zerbe as scout Bill Williams, Cameron Mitchell as Commodore Robert Stockton, Gayle Hunnicutt as Maria Crittenden, and Academy Award–winner F. Murray Abraham as Abe Lincoln.

It was Chamberlain who reportedly pushed for Krige, his love interest in *Wallenberg,* to be his costar in *Dream West.* It was unusual for him to work with the same actress twice in a row and their pairing sparked heated gossip of a developing romance. The rumor mill was in full gear when he took her as his date to an Emmy awards ceremony. Nothing, however, came of their relationship other than some fine acting.

While Alice Krige was a face from Chamberlain's recent past in *Wallenberg,* Fritz Weaver was a reminder of the actor's very beginnings as an actor in *Dr. Kildare.* Weaver, who guest-starred on the medical show, said, "When I met him again after—what?—twenty-five years . . . he hadn't changed—not even physically; he has certainly weathered the years very beautifully."

It wasn't just the way he looked that impressed Weaver. He noted that Chamberlain still possessed "the same sweetness of temper and the same patience under unbelievable pressure—

those long nights of sixteen- or seventeen-hour days when I just blow my cool; he never does," said the veteran actor with admiration. "One time," he recalled, "I can remember him coming over to me and saying, 'It's been a rather trying day, hasn't it?' And when he said this to me the top of my head was about to blow off, and I said, 'Yes, you could put it that way.' It was the only expression of impatience I had seen from him."

Besides remaining calm, Chamberlain never seemed to tire. Or if he did, it rarely showed on his face. And the camera sees everything. "He always looks as if he's had eight hours of sleep, and you know that he's only had two," said Weaver. "He's ready at three o'clock in the morning for his close-up."

Fritz Weaver wasn't the only one to notice how Chamberlain managed to remain physically unaffected by the trials of making a seven-hour production. Anthony Zerbe said, "I worked on the first day of this miniseries . . . then I left. I went away and did another miniseries. I did a play. I went through the Christmas holidays. Four months later I returned to *Dream West* for the final week of filming. Everybody's lost twenty pounds. They're gaunt, they're drawn, they're exhausted. The only person who was totally unchanged was Richard Chamberlain! He's remarkable, and a very sweet man. But he's no different today, on the last day of filming, than he was on October first."

Dream West was a particularly difficult production to make because of so many different location shoots. "You can't find the Old West," explained Chuck McLain. "You've got to put it together in a lot of places." So the *Dream West* company had to pack up and move several times to continue filming in places such as Wyoming, Colorado, Virginia, and Arizona.

Unfortunately for Chamberlain, after making the bulk of his movies and miniseries overseas, his rugged tour of the American landscape went relatively unobserved. "When I'm working in a place I seldom get a chance to see it," he once confided to an interviewer. "It all begins to look like one big movie set. Even the Alps—when we're working there I think, 'Oh, what a great backdrop.'"

In a Richard Chamberlain miniseries, the audience spends more time looking at the actor's face than at the outdoor scenery. There are many among his adoring female fans who would much rather lay their eyes upon his features than gaze upon the Grand Canyon. That doesn't mean, though, that Chamberlain makes an effort to look good in his films. His only concern is to look *right.* And in *Dream West,* looking right often meant looking downright awful. It would be rather impossible to explore the American frontier in the 1830s without getting just a tad dusty, muddy, and sweaty. Chamberlain once said, "I like being dirty . . . and hairy . . . and rotten. It helps me become a different person."

Part of the process of becoming another person was the application of makeup. Michele Burke, who won an Academy Award for her makeup work in *Quest for Fire,* worked on Chamberlain in *Dream West.* But she didn't do all of his makeup. Rather surprisingly, Chamberlain himself took on that responsibility.

"We're all sitting half-asleep in the makeup room," recalled Fritz Weaver, "drinking coffee and he's leaning forward, looking into the mirror, chatting away, but doing his own makeup. . . . He's an expert at it. He has people who work with him; he gets along beautifully with all the makeup people. But there he is, carefully doing it himself. We're used to doing that in the theater," he explained, "but in the movies and TV it's very rare because it's a very specialized art. You have to think about cameras, lenses, what makeup shows where, but he knows all that. He does it and look at him and see the result. And he can make maximum use of his youthful good looks, too, and he knows how to enhance all that with the skill of somebody whose profession it is."

Dream West was aired by CBS on three successive nights in April 1986. Unfortunately, both the script by Evan Hunter and the direction by Dick Lowry were not quite up to the talents of the mini's impressive cast. The story foundered on the rocks of a shallow treatment of history that depended too much upon action scenes and not enough upon character. Critics, by and large, damned the miniseries with faint praise, when they praised it at all, and the TV audience turned to other channels regardless of Chamberlain's supposed drawing power.

Even a king is entitled to an occasional failure. Other show-business kings, such as Elvis Presley and Clark Gable, had their share of flops, too. Chamberlain lost a small measure of his previous clout with the networks, but he was still a miniseries force to be reckoned with.

24

FULL CIRCLE

*P*roof of Chamberlain's standing as King of
the Miniseries was evident when the ac-
tor candidly allowed that he had been offered the starring role
in the ABC blockbuster production, *Amerika,* but turned it
down. "I read it . . . but I just felt it didn't say anything," said
Chamberlain. "It was an awful lot about not very much. I find
that as an actor I'm not very good when I'm not deeply interested in what I'm doing."

Dream West might have been a bust in the ratings, but it
wasn't the major disappointment that *Amerika* had been. He
could certainly be pleased with his good judgment on that
score.

After *Dream West* had finished filming, Chamberlain was
asked about the unusual diversity of characters he had
played. McKeog was a Scotsman, Blackthorne was English,
Wallenberg was Swedish, Frémont was half American and
half French. "Each role has been a different nationality,"
noted the actor. "Some day," he proclaimed, "I want to play
an impassioned Italian. That would be fun."

If the king so wishes, then so it shall be . . . Chamberlain's next project called for him to play the most impassioned Italian of them all, Giacomo Casanova.

Surprisingly, *Casanova* didn't make it to American television as a miniseries. Filmed on location in Italy and Spain, it was broadcast as a three-hour made-for-TV movie on ABC on March 1, 1987. But that wasn't the same movie that was shown on European TV. "There is a great deal of sex in the European version," Chamberlain told author Jim Jerome. "We double-shot a lot. The tits came out, the thighs came out. It was very funny. You'd hear the Velcro go *rrrrip!* and suddenly everybody's naked for the European takes."

The co-executive producer of *Casanova*, Larry Sanitsky, was amused by the judgment of ABC's censors. "We had shot some stuff for Sylvia Kristel who was Emanuelle [the title character of a famous X-rated film], and there was one particular scene where she reveals herself to the young Casanova. To our surprise, the European footage, which we also showed to the network, was considered acceptable for American television."

Besides Kristel, one of the great beauties of international cinema, Ornella Muti, was signed to play yet another bedmate for Casanova, and Chamberlain proclaimed, "I fell in love with her the minute I saw her. The most ravishing woman. Those eyes. I had thousands of scenes with her. But some will be viewed only in Europe."

What a shame.

In addition to Kristel and Muti, *Casanova* boasted a sparkling international cast which included Faye Dunaway, Frank Finlay (the latter two had been his costars in the *Musketeer* films), Sophie Ward, Hannah Schygulla, Roy Kinnear, and Jean-Pierre Cassel.

Despite the parade of beautiful actresses and sexual escapades (most of which were not seen in America), the film's focus stayed squarely on the character of Casanova. Chamberlain saw the title character as "incredibly randy, amazingly resourceful. . . . He fell in love with all the women he went to bed with, but he was incapable of sustaining a relationship. He would like to have found the woman he could have been in love with forever. But he didn't know that being in love and loving were different."

There was more to the Casanova story, though, than his famous trysts. He was, in Chamberlain's words, "a great adventurer coming from eighteenth-century Venice. He was a kind of social genius. He came from an acting family (the lowest of the low at that time) and clawed his way up through society to the very highest echelons.

"The thing that I liked best about Casanova," Chamberlain said, "is that a lot of Don Juan types don't really like women; he loved women. He was crazy about women. He loved everything about them; he loved their underwear, he loved their smell, he loved their laces, he loved their wit. And, of course, he was an extremely sensual guy. . . . He was a great, great lover, but he was mostly his own creation. At the end of his life, he wrote a twelve-volume memoir which is the main source of information about him."

Casanova's autobiography, entitled *History of My Life,* served as the basis of the movie. And perhaps that was the film's problem. It tried at once to be faithful to its source while also attempting to be a tongue-in-cheek sex comedy. Chamberlain said, "The persona is very different from anything else I've played—more fun, more reckless. I don't usually do comedy. And this was very sexy."

Both the sensuality and the humor were somewhat forced. The attempt to double-shoot the film and make two markedly different movies was not altogether successful, at least insofar as the American version was concerned. The film moved along in a herky-jerky fashion as if great bits of important information were missing. And, in fact, the American version of *Casanova* is twenty minutes shorter than the European version and it seems likely that more than breasts and thighs were left on the cutting-room floor when the movie was shown on ABC. Not surprisingly, the reviews were mixed to poor, and the movie was slaughtered in the ratings by its competition, the first night of the Judith Krantz miniseries *I'll Take Manhattan.*

Chamberlain's two television flops were bracketed on either side by two commercial motion picture disasters. In 1985, at the crest of his television popularity, he suddenly appeared in a Cannon Group, Golan and Globus production of *King Solomon's Mines.* The film was crucified by the critics as a poor imitation of Steven Spielberg's Indiana Jones films. For the most part, though, the critics missed the point, seeing the film as a rip-off rather than the spoof that it was. This is not to say that *King Solomon's Mines* was a great movie; it wasn't. But it was much better than the box-office returns would suggest.

Chamberlain was rather effective as Allan Quatermain, the movie's hero. The nice touch throughout the film was that Chamberlain's heroic derring-do was usually ineffectual. He also had quite a few funny lines which he delivered in a dry, understated style. The movie's failure wasn't his. The cheap special effects made the film seem shoddy despite its $12.5 million budget. Worse, though, was the horrendous acting of Chamberlain's costar, Sharon Stone, a former model. She was pretty, but that's about all one can say about her.

Like the *Three* and *Four Musketeers,* the two Allan Quatermain movies were shot at the same time (they were filmed on location in Zimbabwe). The second commercial fiasco, called *Allan Quatermain and the Lost City of Gold* (1987), was even less successful than its predecessor. The critics sneered and it came and went with charitable swiftness. It was much worse than *King Solomon's Mines.*

Before his two Quatermain films, Chamberlain had stayed away from the movies for half of a decade. His last film before the Cannon projects had been a thriller made in Toronto called *Bells* (1980), later retitled *Murder by Phone.* In its own way it was as bad as the Quatermain films, but *Bells* remained a minor embarrassment because it was simply never released for a regular commercial run. It was a silly story about a demented villain who invented a way to kill people through sound waves over the telephone. Chamberlain played a professor who solved the mystery and got the girl in the end.

The 1980s was not Chamberlain's decade for successful movie projects. But in the second half of the 1980s, it seemed as if he had lost his touch not only in the movies, but in theater and television as well.

Two poor TV outings in a row, coupled with the mixed reviews of his *Blithe Spirit* production on Broadway and his two Allan Quatermain movie disasters, made it imperative that the actor come up with a winner—and soon. For his next project, therefore, Chamberlain chose to cast aside his penchant for historical characters and star in a contemporary thriller based on Robert Ludlum's best-selling novel, *The Bourne Identity.*

This two-part, four-hour miniseries was originally intended to be a theatrical film with Burt Reynolds in the title role. But boiling the story down to less than two hours proved no easy task, and eventually the decision was made to turn the book into a two-part, four-hour mini.

Enter Richard Chamberlain. But *The Bourne Identity* marked an important change in the actor's status with the networks. Ever since *Shogun* Chamberlain's name alone had been sufficient as a ratings drawing card. With two losers in a row and the miniseries format itself in trouble, ABC wanted insurance. Rumor had it Leslie-Anne Down was offered the female lead but rejected the part when there was no follow-up offer to hire her husband, cameraman Don Fauntleroy. ABC then turned to popular TV star Jaclyn Smith to play Chamberlain's love interest. And she happily took the role, grateful for the chance to work with an actor of Chamberlain's caliber.

Smith, an actress who rose to fame in the TV series *Charlie's Angels,* never learned her craft the way Chamberlain did after his initial TV success. She nonetheless made the conversion to a popular miniseries star in potboiler productions such as *Windmills of the Gods, Master of the Game,* and *Rage of Angels I* and *II.* Chamberlain and Smith had previously worked together when they cohosted *The Kraft All-Star Salute to Ford's Theater* on CBS in June 1986. Chamberlain was no doubt surprised to learn that she would be his costar in *The Bourne Identity* as well.

But the actor was his usual gentlemanly self, graciously announcing a torrent of praise for his fellow star, saying such things as, "Jaclyn is . . . unselfish, she's a wonderful actress, she's incredibly beautiful, she's warm, she's vulnerable." Jaclyn Smith returned the compliments. "It was a dream to work with Richard," she said earnestly.

The miniseries, which aired on May 8 and 9, 1988, was shot on location in London, Switzerland, and France. The story was complicated and intriguing. Chamberlain described it this way: "The show starts with my character getting shot to pieces in a storm at sea, and falling in the water and practically drowning. He washes up on a Mediterranean island and is saved by a drunken doctor, played wonderfully by Denholm Elliott. Unfortunately, he's shot in the head and can't remember anything," Chamberlain continued. "The only clues to his identity are a Swiss bank account and the fact that he knows all about weapons and martial arts, but he doesn't know why. He discovers shortly that he has fifteen million bucks in the bank and everybody wants to kill him, and he still doesn't know why."

The Bourne Identity was a considerable change of pace for Chamberlain. And, as always, he carried off his role with polished charm, wit, and style. David Bianculli of the New York Post wrote, "For Richard Chamberlain, The Bourne Identity is the latest and most impressive triumph in a long string of ambitious miniseries. In modern dress, playing his most violent and potentially unsympathetic TV role ever, he is excellent." Most critics, in fact, praised Chamberlain, but the mini itself was given mixed reviews. For the most part, critics enjoyed the first installment but felt the story fell apart in the final two-hour segment. For instance, TV Guide said "The storyline becomes a hopeless muddle and only the star power of Richard Chamberlain and a tense, violent conclusion manage to salvage matters." People liked Chamberlain but thought the script was "lazy." Ironically, that bastion of good taste, The New York Times, found the mini to be "vintage television entertainment."

The real test of The Bourne Identity wasn't the critical reaction, it was the audience response. When the ratings came out, there was an almost audible sigh of relief from ABC. The first night of the miniseries was the eleventh-highest-rated show of the week, and the second night hung on for a similar rating. Even more significantly, the thriller was a major winner in the biggest fifteen city markets such as New York, Los Angeles, and Chicago. While The Bourne Identity wasn't a number-one hit like Shogun, it did prove that Chamberlain was still a king with a princely number of followers.

Even as The Bourne Identity was filming in Europe, hot and heavy negotiations were going on in America concerning Chamberlain's possible return to network television in a regular weekly series.

The actor had often said that if the circumstances were right, he might consider returning to series TV. He usually made these pronouncements in such a way as to merely keep the door open without having any intentions of stepping through the opening. But after more than a decade of constant travel and continual farewells to his close friends for massive chunks of time, his attitude about steady work in one, stable location slowly began to change.

After *Dream West,* he said, "Up until now my career has been what made me tick. My goal was to be a fine actor. But in the attempt I was never home. I let a lot of friendships languish. I suddenly realize, after years of wandering around the globe working, I want to be in one place. I want time to nurture friendships, to let people get to know me well. I want to plant something and watch it grow. I'm tired of feeling totally at the mercy of the industry."

He was speaking from the heart, yet old habits were hard to break. *Casanova* in Europe followed, as did *The Bourne Identity.* But the same feelings kept bubbling up from the actor until he plaintively said, "I would *love* to find something I can do and live at home and stay *put* for a while. I'm *tired* of suitcases, I'm *tired* of restaurants, I'm *tired* of all that stuff that most people think are terrific. I just want to stay home."

One of the places Chamberlain has considered home, ever since his big payday for *The Swarm,* is Hawaii. With the end of production of Tom Selleck's *Magnum, P.I.* in the islands in 1988, the television tradition of having a Hawaii-based series appeared to be in jeopardy. Given Chamberlain's desire to stop traveling, his home in America's fiftieth state, and his considerable television appeal, the powerful production company Lorimar entered into negotiations with Chamberlain's agents on the possibility of his starring in a weekly TV series titled *Adam Kane* that would be set in Hawaii.

Chamberlain was genuinely interested. Rumor has it that *Adam Kane,* in its earliest incarnation, was about a doctor (shades of *Dr. Kildare*) who has an interest in New Age phenomena (shades of Richard Chamberlain).

As the negotiations heated up, CBS was brought into the discussions to help try and nail down a deal. The success of *The Bourne Identity* gave Chamberlain considerable leverage in his talks because it proved he was still a potent draw. A deal might have been struck, but the long, drawn-out writers' strike ruined any chances of a fall 1988 start-up for such a series.

It appeared as if the drive to bring Chamberlain back to prime-time weekly TV had been yet another casualty of the strike, but once the picket lines came down, talks between the actor's representatives and Lorimar were quickly resurrected. This time they let nothing get in the way. A tentative deal was soon made; Chamberlain was finally returning to his roots. Though the exact date when *Adam Kane* will premiere was not available as of this writing, the consensus seems to be that it will air sometime in early-to-mid 1989.

The legion of female baby boomers who grew up with a crush on Chamberlain will get their chance to relive a moment of their youth as he once more plays a noble doctor. Sure, those teenage girls may be middle-aged couch potatoes now, but in their hearts both they and Richard Chamberlain will be forever young.

Among modern American actors, there is not a single other performer who has demonstrated the kind of versatility exhibited by Richard Chamberlain. He has starred in four major media: recording, movies, theater, and television. As a singer, he has had hit singles and a hit album. In the movies, he has played everything from farces to thrillers, and from adventure roles to musicals. In the theater, he has mastered Shakespeare and soared with Cyrano. On television, he reached untold millions playing a series of roles, such as Kildare, Blackthorne, and Father Ralph, that will never be forgotten.

Chamberlain has often said that he'd like to play a normal guy, with a wife and family, who has the same sorts of problems that everyone else has. Should the actor receive such a role, it would be the result of casting against type, for his image is so strongly regal. His dignity, his bearing, his commanding voice—all suggest royalty. It's no wonder, really, that Chamberlain has played more than his share of kings and princes. Look at the list: the Prince of Denmark in *Hamlet*, King Richard in *Richard II*, King Edward in *The Woman I Love*, Prince Charming in *The Slipper and the Rose*, and the King of France in *The Man in the Iron Mask*. In addition, there have been lords, counts, Caesars, samurais, and ambassadors. In other words, Chamberlain has created a gallery of characters of noble and heroic proportions. And the vast majority of his creations have had either critical or popular success—or both.

Yet he has never been truly satisfied, either with his career or with his life. In his career, he has sometimes sought stardom and fame, at other times he has sought the quick buck. Most of the time, however, he has pursued excellence. In his personal life, he has struggled to allow himself a greater degree of intimacy. It's a struggle he seems finally to be winning.

Throughout the years, Chamberlain has taken acting just as seriously as Father Ralph took religion. Because of his committment, he has been just as troubled as the priest he played in *The Thorn Birds*, trying to balance his need to work against his strong need for companionship. Like Father Ralph, Chamberlain chose his work—not without some regrets. But now he is intent upon finding a healthy balance between his two needs, and perhaps when that balance is found, Chamberlain will find new reservoirs of emotion that will enrich his acting still further. After all, even with three decades of stardom behind him, there are always new roles, new challenges, in an actor's life.

APPENDICES

Gunsmoke (1959)
Alfred Hitchcock Presents (1959)
Mr. Lucky (1960)
Thriller (1960)
The Deputy (1961)
Rescue 8 (1961)
Bourbon Street Beat (1961)
The Eleventh Hour: Four Feet in the Morning (1963)

TV STARRING ROLES

Dr. Kildare (NBC, 1961–65)
Portrait of a Lady (BBC miniseries, 1968)
Hamlet (Hallmark Hall of Fame, NBC, 1970)
Portrait: The Woman I Love (ABC, 1972)
F. Scott Fitzgerald and "The Last of the Belles" (ABC, 1974)
The Lady's Not for Burning (PBS, 1974)
The Count of Monte Cristo (1976)
The Man in the Iron Mask (1977)
The Good Doctor (PBS, 1978)
Centennial (miniseries, 1979)
Shogun (NBC miniseries, 1980)
1980–81 Tony Awards Show (cohost, 1981)
The Thorn Birds (ABC miniseries, 1983)
Cook and Peary: The Race to the Pole (CBS, 1983)
Wallenberg: A Hero's Story (NBC miniseries, 1985)

The Kraft All-Star Salute to Ford's Theater (CBS, 1986)
Dream West (CBS miniseries, 1986)
Casanova (ABC, 1987)
The Bourne Identity (ABC miniseries, 1988)

MOVIES

The Secret of the Purple Reef (1960)
Cast: Jeff Richards, Margia Dean, Peter Falk, Richard
Chamberlain
Directed by William Witney

A Thunder of Drums (1961)
Cast: George Hamilton, Luana Patten, Richard Boone, Charles
Bronson, Richard Chamberlain, Slim Pickens
Directed by Joseph M. Newman

Twilight of Honor (1963)
Cast: Richard Chamberlain, Nick Adams, Joan Blackman,
Claude Rains, Joey Heatherton, James Gregory, Pat Buttram,
Jeanette Nolan
Directed by Boris Sagal

Joy in the Morning (1965)
Cast: Richard Chamberlain, Yvette Mimieux, Arthur Kennedy,
Sidney Blackmer
Directed by Alex Segal

Petulia (1968)
Cast: Julie Christie, George C. Scott, Richard Chamberlain,
Shirley Knight, Arthur Hill, Joseph Cotton, Pippa Scott,
Kathleen Widdoes
Directed by Richard Lester

The Madwoman of Chaillot (1969)
Cast: Katharine Hepburn, Charles Boyer, Claude Dauphin,
Edith Evans, John Gavin, Paul Henreid, Oscar Homolka,
Margaret Leighton, Giulietta Masina, Nanette Newman, Richard
Chamberlain, Yul Brynner, Donald Pleasence, Danny Kaye
Directed by Bryan Forbes

Julius Caesar (1970)
Cast: Charlton Heston, Jason Robards, John Gielgud, Richard
Johnson, Robert Vaughn, Richard Chamberlain, Diana Rigg,
Jill Bennett, Christopher Lee
Directed by Stuart Burge

The Music Lovers (1971)
Cast: Glenda Jackson, Richard Chamberlain, Max Adrian,
Christopher Gable, Kenneth Colley
Directed by Ken Russell

Lady Caroline Lamb (1972)
Cast: Sarah Miles, Jon Finch, Richard Chamberlain, John
Mills, Margaret Leighton, Ralph Richardson, Laurence Olivier
Directed by Robert Bolt

The Three Musketeers (1974)
Cast: Oliver Reed, Raquel Welch, Richard Chamberlain,
Michael York, Frank Finlay, Christopher Lee, Geraldine
Chaplin, Faye Dunaway, Charlton Heston, Jean-Pierre Cassel,
Roy Kinnear, Spike Milligan
Directed by Richard Lester

The Towering Inferno (1974)
Cast: Steve McQueen, Paul Newman, William Holden, Faye
Dunaway, Fred Astaire, Susan Blakely, Richard Chamberlain,
Jennifer Jones, O.J. Simpson, Robert Vaughn, Robert Wagner,
Susan Flannery
Directed by John Guillermin and Irwin Allen

The Four Musketeers (1975)
Cast: Oliver Reed, Raquel Welch, Richard Chamberlain, Michael York, Frank Finlay, Christopher Lee, Geraldine Chaplin, Faye Dunaway, Charlton Heston, Jean-Pierre Cassel, Simon Ward
Directed by Richard Lester

The Slipper and the Rose (1976)
Cast: Richard Chamberlain, Gemma Craven, Annette Crosbie, Michael Hordern, Margaret Lockwood, Christopher Gable, Kenneth More, Edith Evans
Directed by Bryan Forbes

The Last Wave (1978)
Cast: Richard Chamberlain, Olivia Hamnett
Directed by Peter Weir

The Swarm (1978)
Cast: Michael Caine, Katharine Ross, Richard Widmark, Henry Fonda, Richard Chamberlain, Olivia de Havilland, Fred MacMurray, Ben Johnson, Lee Grant, José Ferrer
Directed by Irwin Allen

Bells (also known as *Murder by Phone*) (1980)
Cast: Richard Chamberlain, John Houseman, Sara Botsford, Robin Gammell, Gary Reineke, Barry Morse
Directed by Michael Anderson

King Solomon's Mines (1985)
Cast: Richard Chamberlain, Sharon Stone, Herbert Lom, John Rhys-Davies, Ken Gampu
Directed by J. Lee Thompson

Allan Quatermain and the Lost City of Gold (1987)
Cast: Richard Chamberlain, Sharon Stone
Directed by J. Lee Thompson

The Philadelphia Story (Florida, 1966)
Private Lives (Ohio and California, 1966)
West Side Story (Long Island, N.Y., 1966)
Breakfast at Tiffany's (New York, 1967)
Hamlet (England, 1969)
The Lady's Not for Burning (England, 1970)
Richard II (Seattle, Los Angeles, and Washington, D.C., 1971–72)
The Fantasticks (Chicago, 1972–73)
Night of the Iguana (Los Angeles and New York, 1976–77)
Fathers and Sons (New York, 1978)
Cyrano de Bergerac (Los Angeles, 1983)
Blithe Spirit (New York, 1987)

RECORDING CAREER

Richard Chamberlain (LP, 1964)
"Three Stars Will Shine Tonight" (a.k.a. "Theme From *Dr. Kildare*"), hit single, 1962
"Love Me Tender," hit single, 1962
"All I Have to Do Is Dream," hit single, 1963
Numerous other singles

INDEX